Warrior • 105

Native American Mounted Rifleman 1861–65

Mark Lardas • Illustrated by Jonathan Smith

First published in Great Britain in 2006 by Osprey Publishing,
Midland House, West Way, Botley, Oxford OX2 0PH, UK
44-02 23rd St, Suite 219, Long Island City, NY 11101, USA
Email: info@ospreypublishing.com

Osprey Publishing is part of the Osprey Group.

Transferred to digital print on demand 2011

First published 2006
1st impression 2006

Printed and bound by PrintOnDemand-Worldwide.com, Peterborough, UK

A CIP catalog record for this book is available from the British Library

ISBN: 978 1 84176 971 4

Page layout by Ken Vail Graphic Design
Index by Glyn Sutcliffe
Maps by John Richards
Originated by The Electronic Page Company, Cwmbran, UK

Dedication
This book is dedicated to William Potter – a first-generation computer scientist, a student of the Civil War,
and my father-in-law.

Acknowledgments
The author wishes to thank the University of Oklahoma Library, the Cherokee Heritage Center and the Smith County
(Texas) Historical Society for their assistance in this work. Special thanks go to Mickel Yantz, Curator of the Cherokee
Heritage Center, who was generous with both illustrations and information. Special thanks also go to my in-laws,
William and Gertrude Potter, who were the source of many of the illustrations.

Author's note
Throughout this text I have used the term "Indians" in favor of the contemporary "Native American" or "aboriginal
peoples". There are several reasons for this, but the chief among them is that "Indians" was the term that was then in use
to describe those whose ancestors came to the North American continent via the Alaskan land bridge during the Ice Age,
rather than those who reached it via boats across the Atlantic or Pacific Oceans following Columbus's expedition in 1492.
In the 19th century Oklahoma was known as the Indian Territory, not the Native American Territory or Aboriginal People's
Territory; the Civil War was not an era noted for political correctness. In a book that attempts to represent the lives of the
Indian soldiers of that war I have opted to stick with then-contemporary language rather than introduce anachronistic
names. The two central characters of this book, George Campbell and Watcher McDonald, are composite characters
based on a number of primary sources and contemporary evidence.

Artist's note
Readers may care to note that the original paintings from which the color plates in this book were prepared are available
for private sale. All reproduction copyright whatsoever is retained by the Publishers. All enquiries should be addressed to:

Jonathan Smith
107 Ryeworth Road
Cheltenham
Gloucestershire
GL52 6LS
UK

Email: jonathanpsmith59@yahoo.co.uk

The Publishers regret that they can enter into no correspondence upon this matter.

The Woodland Trust
Osprey Publishing is supporting the Woodland Trust, the UK's leading woodland conservation charity, by funding
the dedication of trees.

www.ospreypublishing.com

CONTENTS

NATIVE AMERICAN MOUNTED RIFLEMAN 1861–65

INTRODUCTION

When the American Civil War began, independent sovereign nations coexisted within the borders of the United States – the tribes of the indigenous Native Americans who occupied America before the arrival of Europeans. Tribal members were considered citizens of their tribe or nation, rather than citizens of the United States. Some Indian tribes (as they were styled in the 19th century) had been reduced to dependence upon or subservience to the federal government. Other tribes retained their autonomy, which included the right to raise military forces and exclude others from their territories.

The most powerful were the Five Civilized Nations (or Tribes): the Choctaw, Chickasaw, Cherokee, Creek (or Muskogee), and Seminoles. Along with smaller tribes such as the Osage and Delaware, they had assimilated European culture and technology. Often this occurred through intermarriage with those of European and African descent. (By 1860 less than a quarter of the Five Civilized Tribes were full-blooded Indians.) Their children were educated in schools like those of the white citizens of the United States.

The Choctaw and Chickasaw tribes traditionally allied with the United States, siding with the Republic from the Revolutionary era onwards. The Creek and the Seminole historically fought the United States, the Seminole as late as the 1840s. The largest and most advanced

The distribution of Indian tribes in and around the Indian Territory. (Author's collection)

nation, the Cherokee, had allied with Britain during the American Revolution. Thereafter, they fought on the same side of the battlefield as the new republic.

In the 1830s and 1840s these Indians left their ancestral homelands east of the Mississippi. Some left voluntarily, but most were forced to go by a federal government which sided with the Southern states that wanted these lands for white immigrants. Their old lands taken, the Indians built a new civilization in the Indian Territory (today's Oklahoma and southeastern Kansas). Between relocation and the Civil War they transformed the region into the richest part of the United States west of the Mississippi. They built plantations, farms, and ranches, dug mines, and graded turnpikes. They created the first public school system in the United States. They had the highest rate of literacy west of the Mississippi. Most literate Indians could read and write in two languages – English and their native tongue. They printed bilingual newspapers, using alphabets they had derived. Most had become Christians. Each nation had written constitutions and elected representative tribal governments.

The Civilized Tribes drew heavily on the white Southerners' lifestyle. Wealthy Indians established plantations, some requiring hundreds of black slaves to work them. Their houses were among the finest in the nation. One wealthy Choctaw owned a fleet of steamboats that carried agricultural products from the Indian Territory to white markets on the Mississippi River and goods back to the Indian Territory.

Indians of the Five Civilized Nations lived in a manner that the frontier whites would respect. They built log cabins. Their towns held gristmills, cotton gins, blacksmith shops, and warehouses, which were run by Indians, generally the mixed-bloods. By 1860 they were finally beginning to receive the long-promised payments for the eastern lands they had been forced to abandon. The inhabitants of the Indian Territory satisfied all of the requirements for statehood – except that of being United States citizens.

Fault lines of discontent existed in these tribes. The biggest was caused by removal. Some tribal members who had believed relocation was inevitable, signed treaties with the whites, got the best deal they could negotiate, and left voluntarily. Others opposed relocation and sought redress through the courts. They regarded those who had signed treaties as turncoats who had undercut their brothers by signing agreements to vacate the land.

Their anger was exacerbated because the "treaty Indians" who had arrived in the Indian Territory first, got the best land. The larger, anti-removal faction, arriving after futile legal battles which dissipated much of their wealth, had to settle on what was left. The problem was compounded as the federal government forced other, more primitive, tribes into the Indian Territory, reducing the available territory still further. The Cherokee and Creek Nations fought civil

Indian leaders lived in houses in Park Hill much like the pictured Murell House. Built in 1845, the Murell House was not the grandest building in the Cherokee town, but survived because a white Indian Agent owned it. He fell outside the bounds of the Cherokee Nation's fratricidal conflict. (Library of Congress, Prints and Photographs Division)

A soldier of the Union Indian Brigade in 1862, as depicted by an artist for Frank Leslie's *Illustrated Weekly*. (Potter Collection)

OPPOSITE Black Beaver, a Delaware, served as a scout in the United States Army during both the Mexican–American War and the Civil War. During the Civil War, he guided Union garrisons out of the Indian Territory at the beginning of the war. Chased out of his home in Fort Washita for his Union sympathies, he fought for the North during the rest of the war. (NARA)

wars during the 1840s as treaty and anti-removal factions settled scores by resorting to arson and assassination. The US government enforced peace in the 1850s, but the scars were still fresh when the Civil War broke out.

A second fault line was that formed by Indians who preferred to follow traditional ways versus those who assimilated the white lifestyle. The traditional Indians, generally the full-blooded minority, lived in cabins, eschewed the towns for the forests, and made their living through hunting, fishing, and trapping, rather than agriculture. The assimilating Indians adopted European technology, and exchanged tradition for positions generating wealth and influence. In some tribes – particularly the Choctaw and Chickasaw – assimilation was almost complete. In others, especially the Cherokee, the Seminole, and Creek, the traditionalists were important.

As in the United States, slavery created a third contentious fault line. Many Indians adopted chattel slavery, but others were staunchly abolitionist. The Seminoles were the most conflicted by slavery, as they intermarried with runaway black slaves while in Florida. However, the Creeks and Cherokee also had strong anti-slavery factions, especially among the full-bloods and those most strongly opposing relocation.

When the several states of the Confederacy severed ties with the Union, the Five Civilized Tribes had to make a decision – whether to stay neutral or whether to align with the northern states of the Union or those of the southern Confederacy. Economically and culturally the decision-makers for these nations were tied to the South. The South courted these nations, while the North abandoned its forts in the Indian Territory.

Some tribes, notably the Choctaw and Chickasaw, eagerly declared for the Confederacy. The Creeks, Cherokees, and then the Seminoles were swept along by the Confederate tide started by these tribes. Finally, smaller tribes were given a choice between joining the Confederacy or being destroyed by their larger Indian neighbors. Most fell in line. Imitating their white neighbors, the Indian Nations created armies on the European model, organized into companies, battalions, and regiments.

Individual tribal members were also forced to declare for one side or the other. Neutrality was not tolerated, and those that would not declare for Dixie were driven out. Refugees in Kansas, they took up arms in Union regiments to reclaim their homes. The stage was set for the appearance of one of the Civil War's most exotic and tragic warriors – the Indian mounted rifleman.

Their story is told through the eyes of two composite Cherokee participants: George Campbell, and Agatisgv, or Watcher McDonald. Both are young men, and second cousins. George, who is $\frac{5}{8}$ ths white, represents the mixed-bloods, and joins a Confederate unit, Watie's Mounted Rifles. Watcher, pure Cherokee, is swept into the Union's 2nd Kansas Indian Home Guard Regiment.

CHRONOLOGY

1860

December 20   South Carolina becomes the first state to secede from the United States.

1861

February 1   Texas secedes.

February 4   The Confederacy is formed and begins a constitutional convention in Montgomery, Alabama. The first states to join the Confederacy are North and South Carolina, Georgia, Florida, Alabama, Mississippi, Louisiana, and Texas.

February 7   Choctaw Nation affirms amity with the Confederacy.

February 17   Inter-tribal council called to discuss the relations that the Five Civilized Tribes will have with the United States and the Confederacy.

April 12   Confederate forces fire on Fort Sumter.

April 15   President Lincoln declares a state of insurrection and sends out a call for volunteers.

May 4   United States withdraws army garrisons in Indian Territory posts.

May 6   Arkansas secedes.

May 25   Chickasaw Nation declares independence and allies with the Confederacy.

June 14   Choctaw Nation declares its independence, allies with the Confederacy, and authorizes formation of a regiment.

July 12   Stand Watie raises a private Cherokee battalion of Mounted Rifles for the Confederacy.

July 24   1st Choctaw and Chickasaw Mounted Rifle Regiment completes mustering.

August 1   Seminole Nation joins the Confederacy.

August 10   Battle of Wilson's Creek. Watie's 1st Cherokee Volunteers participate on Confederate side.

August 17   Creek Mounted Rifle regiments are organized by the pro-Confederate faction of the Creek Nation.

August 26   Cherokee Nation declares war on the United States.

September 19   Seminole Mounted Rifle battalion organized.

October 4   A Cherokee regiment (Drew's Mounted Rifles) raised. Many members are Union loyalists.

November 15   Loyal Creeks and Seminoles led by Opothleyohola begin retreat to Kansas.

November 19   Battle of Round Mountain. Confederates attack the pro-Union Creek and Seminole Indians.

December 9   Battle of Chusto-talasah (or Bird Creek).

December 26   Battle of Chustenahalan – loyalist Indians driven from Indian Territory.

1862

March 7–8   Battle of Pea Ridge – Indian regiments participate.

April 4   1st and 2nd Indian Home Guard Regiments (USA) authorized.

June 21   First Indian Expedition begins. Union forces enter Cherokee Nation from Fort Scott.

July 14   Union forces capture Tahlequah, the Cherokee capital.

July 16   The Cherokee Nation declares for the Union, then splits into Union and Confederate factions. Drew's Mounted Rifles (CSA) deserts and is later reorganized as the 3rd Indian Home Guard Regiment (USA).

July 18   Union captures Fort Gibson.

July 19   White Union troops evacuate the Cherokee Nation.

July 28   After the withdrawal of white Union troops, Indian Home Guard regiments are forced to retreat back to Kansas. First Indian Expedition ends.

October 10   Second Indian Expedition begins.

October 22   Battle of Old Fort Wayne, at Beattie's Prairie, Indian Territory.

October 23   Pro-Union Indians at the Wichita Agency revolt against the Confederacy and flee to Kansas.

October 30   Battle of Newtonia. Indian units participate on both sides.

December   Union Indians capture Forts Gibson and Davis from Confederate forces. Fort Davis destroyed by Union.

1863

February 3   Northern Cherokees emancipate Negro slaves owned by Cherokees.

May   Union reoccupies Fort Gibson and holds it for the rest of the war.

July 1–2   Battle of Cabin Creek. Union victory secures Fort Gibson's supply line.

July 4   Gettysburg ends and Vicksburg surrenders.

July 17	Battle of Honey Springs seriously weakens Confederates.
August 21	Quantrill sacks Lawrence, Kansas.
September 1	Union forces occupy Fort Smith, Arkansas.
October 6	Battle of Baxter Springs cuts supply lines to Fort Gibson.
December 16	Quantrill's attack on Fort Gibson repulsed.
1864	
February 15	Battle of Middle Boggy Depot.
April 18	Battle of Poison Springs, Arkansas. Chickasaw and Choctaw regiments participate.
June 15	Steamboat *J.R.Williams* captured by Confederate Indians while carrying supplies to Fort Gibson.
August 22	Atlanta falls.
September 19	2nd battle of Cabin Creek. Union supply train captured.
November 8	Lincoln reelected.
1865	
April 3	Richmond falls to the Union.
April 9	Lee surrenders at Appomattox.
May 26	Kirby-Smith sends Confederate troops right into the Trans-Mississippi.
June 18	Choctaw Nation ceases hostilities.
June 23	Stand Watie surrenders his command. Cherokee, Creek, and Seminole Nations cease hostilities.
July 16	Chickasaw Nation ceases hostilities.
1866	
April 28	Choctaw and Cherokee Nations sign peace treaties with the United States.
July 19	Cherokee Nation signs a peace treaty with the United States.

Indian Territory during the Civil War.

DON'T MISS OUT ON THE GLORY: RECRUITMENT, ENLISTMENT, AND TRAINING

On May 25, 1861 the Chickasaw Nation declared independence from the United States. The sixth resolution of that declaration stated that the governor of the Chickasaw Nation was "instructed to issue his proclamation to the Chickasaw Nation … calling upon the Chickasaw warriors to form themselves into volunteer companies of such strength and with such officers (to be chosen by themselves) as the governor may prescribe, to report themselves by filing their company rolls at the Chickasaw Agency and to hold themselves, with the best arms and ammunition, together with a reasonable supply of provisions, in readiness at a minute's warning to turn out, under the orders of the commanding general of the Chickasaws …"

It differed little from similar proclamations issued throughout the Confederate states, and was the first of many similar ordinances passed by the Civilized Tribes authorizing the organization of formal military units. Like volunteer units created by the states on both sides, the Indian Nations adopted a European military model: a regiment with around ten companies of 100 men each.

Except for the first regiment created – the 1st Choctaw and Chickasaw Mounted Rifles – individual Indian Nations raised and organized these Confederate units. Each tribal government in turn formally severed ties with the United States and allied with the Confederacy.

Smaller tribes such as the Seminole and Osage that could not raise a full regiment of ten organized companies, arranged them into battalions of three to five companies. The largest nations – the Creek and Cherokee – each initially created two regiments. A formal unit formed by members of the minor tribes which had been forced to declare war on the United States was raised, but fell apart. Unenthusiastic about an alliance that included Texas, Indian members from more primitive tribes (Comanche, Kiowa, and Kickapoo) left when they felt like it, while Indians from more advanced tribes (Delaware and Wichita) deserted Confederate service and fled to Kansas.

Confederate enlistment

For someone like George Campbell, actually joining a Confederate Indian unit was simple. The Civilized Nations were divided into administrative and legislative districts. Companies in tribal regiments were organized by district, so men simply went to the nearest public building in a district and enrolled. The recruiting site might be a local school, a church, or a council hall.

Once enough men had signed up, officers were elected. Each company required a captain, a first lieutenant, and two second lieutenants. As with white militia companies throughout the United States, becoming an officer in an Indian regiment was more a function of political skill than military experience. A reputation as a fighter helped, but only if you convinced the men in your company that this made you the best leader. The companies were then mustered into a regimental formation, and the volunteers were formally enrolled. That was it.

Initially the Confederate units were made up of volunteers who agreed to serve for one year. When 1861 became 1862 and the war showed no signs of ending, most units allowed their members to reenlist for one more year. By the summer of 1863, when the Union Army occupied half of the Indian Territory, manpower shortages became common. Each Indian Nation allied with the Confederacy passed a conscription law, making military service mandatory for all males between the ages of 15 and 50. They also lengthened the terms of service to three years or the duration of the war.

George chose to join what in 1861 was the 2nd Cherokee Mounted Rifles, also known as Watie's Mounted Rifles. It was created from a smaller, existing unit, the Cherokee Volunteers, a force privately raised by Stand Watie, a strongly pro-Confederacy Cherokee politician. It fought alongside the Confederate Army at Wilson's Creek before the Cherokee Nation entered the war. George enlisted for one year and enrolled as a private.

The decision was a simple one for George. Thirty years earlier the whites of the Confederate States drove the Cherokee and other Civilized Tribes from the Indian lands east of the Mississippi because the Indians were not regarded as good enough to live beside whites. Now the Confederacy was offering an alliance that treated his nation, his family and himself as equals to the white Confederates. They were inviting the Indians to join them in battle – the place where George thought the greatest honor was to be found. By contrast, the North had withdrawn its garrisons from the Indian Territory, leaving the Civilized Tribes at the mercy of Plains nomads and asking nothing more than the Indians stay at home, tending their farms. That was fine for women, but men, in George's view, should prove themselves on the field of battle.

Further, George's family owned black slaves. Should the North win, black abolitionists were bound to come to the Indian Territory and deprive his family of their labor force and thus a large part of the family's wealth. They might even insist on treating the slaves as equals to the Cherokee, something George could not fathom. In his view, it was better to fight than to meekly accept that.

Indian regiments, like those elsewhere in the Civil War, ran on paper as much as they did on bullets, beans, and forage. This is the monthly return of the 2nd Creek Mounted Rifle Regiment. Paper was often harder to obtain in the Indian Territory than gunpowder. (Author's collection)

Union enlistment

For Watcher McDonald, enlisting in the Union Army was more complicated. At 17 years old Watcher had become an orphan. An epidemic killed his family while Watcher was off at his final year at school. After graduating, he changed his inheritance and lived at the family cabin, hunting and trapping enough to meet his needs. He disliked slavery, preferring to prosper through his own labor. Watcher was uninterested in the wider world or the white man's war, and simply wanted a peaceful life at home. His major ambition was to accumulate enough cattle so that he could support the daughter of a neighboring Cherokee as his wife and raise a family.

While the Confederacy actively recruited the Civilized Nations, the Union began the war by pulling its garrisons out of the Indian Territory, and began preparing to send Kansas troops into Missouri and Arkansas to hold those states for the Union. A few abolitionist cranks promised the loyalist Indians support, but Washington had enough on its plate without worrying about pro-Union Indians on the edge of nowhere. It was not until the Confederate Indians pushed a flood of loyalist Indians into Kansas that the Union began focusing attention on this Indian problem.

The area around Fort Scott became flooded with Indian refugees. Thousands had to be fed and clothed and the North did a poor job of it. The neighbor and the daughter that Watcher had been sweet on were among those that died of hunger and disease at Fort Scott during the winter of 1861/62. Among these refugees were hundreds of men of fighting age who wanted to return home. They needed weapons. They petitioned Washington for the tools to retake their homes. The United States Army was fighting the Sioux and Blackfoot in Kansas and Nebraska and opposed arming Indians – even civilized Indians. By 1862, however, Washington decided that arming loyalist Indians, and allowing them to return to the Indian Territory was cheaper than feeding refugees. A Confederate Indian Brigade had fought at Pea Ridge, so organized and armed Indian units already existed.

The state of Kansas was authorized to raise five Home Guard regiments from pro-Union Indians. Initially, two Indian Home Guard regiments were organized in May 1862. The regimental officers, as well as some of the company officers, were whites, who received commissions from the state of Kansas. Some of the Indians also received commissions, but as with the white officers, the commissions were issued by Kansas, not their nation.

These regiments mixed Indians from different tribes together. Creeks, Seminoles, and Plains Indians tended to enlist in the 1st Home Guard Regiment, while the Cherokee and Osage predominated in the 2nd Home Guard. The Indians who enlisted in 1862 were primarily refugees from the Indian Territory. Others, notably Delaware Indians, had been living in Kansas, and had served the Union Army as scouts prior to the organization of the Indian Home Guard units.

By the spring of 1862 Watcher McDonald was among the refugees at Fort Scott. He had considered joining Drew's Mounted Rifles, a Cherokee regiment raised for the Confederacy, but consisting of anti-slavery full-bloods who wanted to defend the Cherokee Nation from all comers, North or South. Watcher's decision to remain at home was overtaken by events. When loyal Creeks and Seminoles were driven out of the Indian Territory their path took them near his cabin. Forced to choose sides, Watcher opted to side with the loyalists, many of whom were anti-slavery full-bloods like him. Having lost his home, and wishing to win it back, Watcher enlisted in the 2nd Indian Home Guard Regiment.

The Delaware had been traditional allies of the United States since the American Revolution. At the start of the Civil War one branch of the tribe lived in Kansas, and a second branch lived near Fort Washita, near the Red River. The Delaware served as scouts – pictured here – and enlisted in the Union Indian Brigade. (Potter Collection)

Training

Neither George nor Watcher spent much time training. In all likelihood neither spent *any* time training. The common belief held by both whites and Indians was that Indians were born warriors, who needed no instruction.

Virtually every Indian who joined a Civil War unit possessed the minimum skills required of a soldier, acquired after a life spent on the frontier. They could handle firearms and shoot well; they could ride a horse; they could track and follow a trail. Shooting, riding, and tracking were all skills needed for hunting, and most of the Civilized Indians hunted both for subsistence and for pleasure.

Indian troops also knew how to live on campaign. They knew how to set up a tent, and establish a camp with the latrines downstream of the drinking water. Many traditionalists preferred lean-tos to cabins. The Indians that adopted white ways still camped occasionally, even if it was only when driving herds of cattle or horses to market.

The Five Civilized Tribes had long martial traditions: the Chickasaw were known as the "Spartans of America." Creek Red Sticks had faced Andrew Jackson's militia at Horseshoe Bend, and the Seminole had fought the United States Army and Marine Corps to a standstill in Florida.

In truth, the belief that every Indian was born a warrior was a conceit. The last Seminole War sputtered out in the 1840s, so the youngest Seminole warrior that fought in it was in his thirties when the Civil War started. The war leaders themselves were in their fifties and sixties. The last wars fought by the other four tribes took place between 1810 and 1825 and a generation had reached manhood, and raised children to the edge of adulthood since then. In those intervening years the people of those tribes had transformed from Spartan warriors to successful farmers, ranchers, and businessmen.

Most Indian soldiers, secure in the belief that they were born soldiers who needed no training, never progressed beyond the armed posse stage. They became highly skilled at some aspects of warfare: they were incomparable raiders, and deadly snipers. But neither side could get Indian troops to mount guard, patrol defensively, or mount garrison duty.

The problem went up the ranks, as well. Officers were likely to be politicians, business owners, or light-horse commanders, not soldiers. (The light-horse was the law enforcement organization of the Five

In addition to the Indian regiments in the Trans-Mississippi, many Indians east of the Mississippi enlisted on both sides of the conflict. These casualties are Indian sharpshooters of the Union Army, wounded in the second battle of Fredericksburg. Many Northern Indians, especially Chippewa from Michigan, enlisted as sharpshooters. (Library of Congress, Prints and Photographs Division)

Civilized Tribes with duties comparable to the law-enforcement responsibilities of the Texas Rangers.) The true war leaders, with experience of combat, were generally too old to take to the field.

The officers were not stupid, merely uneducated in the ways of military leadership. Unlike the battlefields to the East, there was no cadre of West Point professionals from which they could learn. The books on tactics and drill churned out by the presses of New York City and Richmond, which amateur officers in Virginia and Mississippi studied, rarely found their way to the Indian Territory. Instead, Indian officers learned basic concepts such as securing an objective, or posting pickets through experience, and that experience was often gained the hard way after the enemy exploited an opportunity produced by ignorance of a particular idea.

Many Indian officers learned quickly. Some, like Stand Watie, proved to have an instinctive skill for tactics, becoming masters of mounted combat. No Indian officer, nor any white officer in the Indian Territory, Confederate or Union, developed an aptitude for strategy or a grand strategy for victory in the Indian Territory. This condemned the region to four years of reactive warfare.

These limitations were not exclusive to Indian troops, nor were they "racial" characteristics. Virtually every white frontier volunteer committed to the Indian Territory shared the same shortcomings as the Indian troops. Frontiersmen in Texas and Kansas, and the backwoods farmer of western Arkansas and Missouri had backgrounds similar to Indians of the Civilized Tribes. White officers committed to the Indian Territory were also amateurs. They too regarded themselves as born warriors who needed no training to become outstanding soldiers. As a result, they formed units similar to the Indian Mounted Rifle regiments with similar strengths and shortcomings. The officers were amateurs and the men undisciplined.

Cherokee Stand Watie proved to be one of the outstanding amateur soldiers of the Civil War. Starting with no military experience, he became the only Indian to receive a general's commission during the war. (Author's collection)

THE MOUNTED RIFLEMAN: APPEARANCE

George Campbell's appearance was rather less formal than on his enlistment, although possibly a little more formal than during his training. For the Confederate Indians, it was a "come-as-you-are" war. The Confederacy promised their Indian allies weapons, equipment, and money. Some money came in the first year, but the promised weapons and supplies only trickled in. They were sent, but most disappeared en route, absorbed to serve the equally urgent needs of white regiments from Texas and Arkansas.

During the first year of the war George provided his own clothing. He packed up his most rugged jacket and trousers, store-bought items, because George came from a family of property. They were the same clothes that he would use for outdoor work, whether it was the spring branding at an uncle's ranch or supervising repairs to his father's warehouse.

13

He wore a homespun shirt – cloth-making was a cottage industry among the Cherokee, just as it was with the other Civilized Tribes – and he kept a couple of spare shirts and drawers in his pack, along with an extra pair of trousers.

He also wore a cravat tied around his neck. This was a tie intended for show, not a bandana. A man had to keep up appearances when he went to war. He also wore his best riding boots – calf-high leather boots that had been made for him when he turned 18, and carefully cleaned and polished since then.

He topped the outfit with a beaver hat. Not the fancy beaver he wore when he went courting, but a sturdy, wide-brimmed hat that would repel water when it rained and keep the summer sun off his face and neck. Other men in his regiment favored a straw hat. It was cooler in the summer, but George thought that a straw hat was not quite the thing to wear on a glorious cavalry charge. He stuck a feather in it – not the hawk or eagle feather the full-bloods used, but a fancy peacock feather to show that while he might be a private, he was still a cavalier.

On the advice of a friend, he had brought along a gourd canteen and a small backpack to store his clothes and possessions. His father made him take a blanket roll to sleep in, and an oilcloth raincoat. His mother gave him a wooden plate (less likely to break than her china or earthenware), a spoon, a comb, and a small Bible. He was under instructions to read it every day. At first it sat in the bottom of his pack until the day before a battle, when it would come out briefly before returning until the eve of the next fight. By the third year of the war, George fell into the habit of reading it regularly.

E.C. Boudinot was a cousin of Stand Watie. He served as an officer in Watie's regiment, and was later the Cherokee delegate to the Confederate Congress. (Library of Congress, Prints and Photographs Division)

George wore war paint in his first few battles. His grandfather showed him the patterns that a Cherokee warrior would wear, but it struck George as something that belonged to an earlier age, like going to war wearing knee-britches and a tricorn hat. Others in his company used it in the battles against the renegade Creeks and Cherokees that sided with the Northern abolitionists, so George went along with the tradition. He also wore paint at the big battle at Pea Ridge because he wanted the Yankees to know that they were facing Indian warriors. A few of the other men carried things too far – scalping some of the Yankees they killed at that fight. Afterwards George decided that paint was too much trouble, and regarded it as rather old-fashioned.

By the time he was reading his Bible regularly, his store-boughts had worn out. In fact most of his outfit was ready for the rag-box. By then most of the stores in the Cherokee Nation had been burned down, and the stores in the Choctaw Nation or northern Texas were bare. At first he had made do with spare clothing salvaged when his family fled the Cherokee Nation for the Red River. When those ran out, he was reduced to salvaging what he could find on the battlefield or

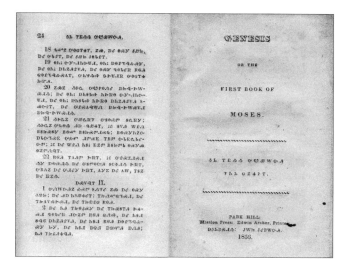

George Campbell's historical counterparts likely carried a Bible similar to this one, which was written in Cherokee, and published in Park Hill, Cherokee Nation, in 1858. (Cherokee Heritage Center)

from successful raids. His trousers had come from a Kansas cavalryman that George had captured, and his shirts from a Union supply wagon that his company had taken.

He had gone through two pairs of footwear. When his riding boots gave out he found a dead artilleryman with the same size feet. Then he helped capture a Union officer's baggage and the man's calf-high riding boots ended up as George's share of the loot. In the summer of 1863 he decided that comfort was more important than looks and replaced his beaver with a hat of woven palmetto.

George renewed the rest of his kit in a similar manner, except for his coat. After his fiancée had sewn corporal's stripes on the jacket, it became a talisman. He kept it until the war ended, patching it, and replacing the buttons with acorns and wood chips. By war's end, the coat had first-sergeant's stripes on it.

George was as well dressed as his officers at the war's outset, and probably a little better dressed than them when it ended. They, too, went to war in their civilian clothing, and remained so dressed for the rest of the war.

Between August 1861, when George enlisted, and June 1864, when Stand Watie sent George's regiment home, George received no clothing or equipment from the Confederacy. A few of his comrades received an item or two if they were stationed close to the Texas or Arkansas border, for example, but the majority, like George, received nothing. The Indian Nations occasionally issued clothing, but typically it was of the meanest quality. George Grayson, who served in a Creek regiment, related that his government-issued hats of undressed wool that were crudely assembled, smelled like a sheep pen, and soon lost their shape. The brim would flop down, and the hat popped into a cone shape at the least provocation. Other issue clothing was probably of comparable quality.

Watcher McDonald had an easier time getting his uniform and equipment than George Campbell. The Union Army issued some of his clothing, as well as personal equipment. Watcher had joined the retreating Creek Indians before the battle of Chusto-talasah (Bird Creek), and did not have a family to look after. He arrived at Fort Scott, Kansas, with his rifle, the clothes on his back, and a few other possessions that he had managed to stow in a bag. He still had his horse, which made him a rich man by the standards of most refugees.

The United States Army had been using Indian Scouts for many years. Although the Indian Home Guard regiments were intended as regular units, the army initially outfitted them in the same way as Indian Scouts. Watcher received a black Hardee hat and a navy-blue four-button sack coat. The coat was trimmed in infantry blue, even though the unit intended to fight a mounted war. The coat was too large for Watcher, but since the clothing issued to the Indians only seemed to come in the sizes of too large or too small, Watcher decided that there were more advantages to extra space than there were to an undersized jacket.

The hat came without a branch insignia, or regiment number and company letter. As with many other Indians in the Home Guard, Watcher stuck a pair of hawk's feathers into the hatband – to declare his identity as an Indian, and to proclaim his warrior status.

In the first months after the Indian Home Guard was raised, only Indian officers, who like the white officers had to buy their outfits, wore any other piece of a Union uniform other than the Hardee hat and sack coat. Those were the only two pieces of uniform that the army issued the Union Indians. The only exceptions were Indians who "found" additional pieces in an unguarded quartermaster store. Watcher took advantage of those occasions to add a knapsack in which he could store his possessions, a new canteen to replace the worn-out wooden canteen he had brought with him, and some horse blankets. Those that did not go on his horse he used to keep himself warm at night.

Being issued only a hat and coat was not a hardship to the occasional Kiowa who enlisted. They did not mind fighting barelegged, and in a coat with no shirt underneath. Initially, it did not cause Watcher or the Delawares who enlisted trouble – they simply used the civilian trousers and shirts that they had owned prior to enlisting. Even those Delawares who had fled the Wichita Agency could rely on relatives in the Delaware Reservation in Kansas to supply them with clothes. But many of the Creeks, Seminoles, and Cherokees who fled to Kansas were wearing rags when they arrived. They had no source of additional clothing, no cloth to make clothing, no thread to weave cloth, and no money to purchase cloth, thread, or clothing.

Initially, the Union Army met the needs of these Indians in a time-honored manner: looting the enemy. When Confederate military stores were captured, the Indians were allowed to keep everything except military supplies. The Confederacy had its own difficulties clothing its soldiers in the Trans-Mississippi region. Virtually every stock of clothing found in captured Confederate quartermaster stores or supply wagons in western Arkansas and Missouri consisted of civilian clothing collected for use by their troops there. Just as the Confederate Indians clothed themselves with captured Union uniforms late in the war, in 1862 the Union Indians wore captured Confederate clothing. Unfortunately, these opportunities were few.

Watcher took advantage of one windfall after the battle of Locust Grove. A Union column that included the Indian Brigade captured a 60-wagon Confederate train filled with powder and supplies near Locust Grove. The powder and military stores went to the army, but the captured clothes were civilian clothing. Watcher was able to get some new trousers and a pair of spare shirts. Later in the war, in 1863 and after the period when the Union held Fort Gibson, Watcher was able to

Officers of the Union Indian Brigade: Lt. Col. Lewis Downing (left) and Capt. James Vann, of the 3rd Regt. Indian Home Guard, both Cherokees. Like white officers, they purchased their own uniforms. (US Army Military History Institute)

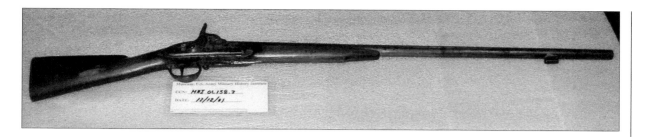

get clothing issued by the army. This proved critical because the local weaving industry that existed in the Cherokee Nation (and all the Civilized Nations) before the war was completely disrupted by raids and counter-raids. As his civilian clothes wore out Watcher received military issue – everything from trousers and a greatcoat, to underwear like socks and drawers.

Footgear, and other leather equipment was a similar problem for Watcher. At first he wore moccasins that he had made. When they wore out, he either made new ones in his spare time, or depended upon army-issue boots or brogans. The army-issue footwear never fitted as well or felt as comfortable as his own moccasins, but there were times when that was all he had.

As the war dragged on Watcher and his companions became scruffier in their appearance. Fort Gibson remained in a state of semi-siege from late 1863 until the spring of 1865. Food and ammunition had a higher priority than clothing, and clothing for the Indian units had the lowest priority of all.

This shotgun was converted from an army flintlock musket. Fitted with a percussion lock and a cut-down stock, it was typical of the type of weapon used by Confederate forces. (United States Military Heritage Institute)

EQUIPMENT

George Campbell's equipment was as informal as his uniform. He brought his own weapons, horse, and tack. George was lucky enough to come from a well-to-do family. His father owned several rifles, shotguns, and pistols. George, as the oldest son, was sent off in fine style, with one of the hunting rifles – a surplus army flintlock that had been converted to use percussion caps – an old single-shot pistol, and a side-knife. The muzzle-loading long-arm had started out as a smoothbore but had been rifled at the same time that the flintlock had been replaced. The pistol, too, was a muzzle-loader, but his father had not wanted to part with the revolver. A blacksmith in the town near where the family lived had made the side-knife from a file, adding a wooden handle and a D-shaped guard.

A museum recreation of the Bisco and Short workroom, where Texas rifles were manufactured. The tool chest and workbenches came from the Tyler Armory, and show the piecework nature of the work done there. (Smith County Historical Society)

George's weapons were similar to those of his companions. Perhaps two thirds of the Confederate Indian soldiers brought their own arms into the service. While the Confederate government promised their Indian allies weapons, only a few ever arrived. In August 1863, of the 2,800 long-arms in one Indian Brigade, nearly 70% were personal weapons that soldiers had brought with them when they enlisted. Over half of these were shotguns, and 21% were old smoothbore muskets. About 800 had been supplied by the Confederacy and over half of these weapons (450) were "Texas" rifles, hand-made at an armory in Tyler, Texas. Hunting rifles came in sizes as varied as the soldiers. George Grayson, a soldier in one of the Creek regiments, stated in his memoirs that one of the soldiers in his company went into battle with a squirrel rifle.

The shotgun proved the weapon of choice for Confederate Indians. A shotgun was rugged and reliable. When the barrel was sawed down it could be wielded with one hand, making it an ideal cavalry weapon. Loaded with heavy buckshot it made a formidable weapon in a charge. George kept his rifle only through his first campaign – the winter campaign against Opothleyohola's Union loyalists. George found it difficult to handle a rifled-musket on horseback, in broken or woody terrain.

A Yankee revolver that George "found" during the battle of Pea Ridge replaced George's single-shot pistol. While a long-arm was considered essential, many Confederate Indians carried revolvers and pistols as well. As with the long-arms, most were the personal possessions of the individual soldier, brought from home. They were varied enough to equip a firearms museum, and ranged from ancient dueling pistols to modern Colt revolvers. George Grayson reported that one of his comrades had an old horse pistol – probably an old Dragoon Colt, dating back to the Mexican–American War. As with uniforms and other supplies the Confederate Indians often upgraded their armament with pistols scavenged from the Yankees on the battlefield.

The Confederate government did send the Indians lead, gunpowder, cartridges, and percussion caps. Gunpowder was generally available in sufficient quantities, especially early in the war. Percussion caps and cartridge paper were always in short supply, however. As early as April 1862 Stand Watie's regiment was so short of percussion caps that he sent an express rider to Fort Smith to collect some.

These shortages were not due to Confederate discrimination against their Indian allies. Rather, they reflected shortages experienced throughout the Confederacy, compounded by the distance of the Indian Territory from sources of supply. When the Civil War started there were

No Confederate Indian, and few that fought for the Union, would have been without a side-knife. This example was presented to Stand Watie, and used by him during the Civil War. (Cherokee Heritage Center)

no railroads in northern Texas, Louisiana, or western Arkansas. Supplies came by riverboat or wagon train. River travel was reliable only as far as the periphery of the Indian Territory – Fort Smith on the eastern border of the territory and the Red River on its southern boundary. From there, supplies were moved by pack or wagon train.

The problem was compounded because the states surrounding the Indian Territory also needed to equip and supply their own units. The Confederacy had promised their Indian allies weapons from the Little Rock Arsenal. Instead the promised weapons – smoothbore muskets that dated to the War of 1812 – were distributed to Arkansas regiments by the state's legislature.

One thing that Confederate Indians had in sufficient numbers were the large side-knives they carried. As much a tool as a weapon, side-knives – often called Bowies or "Arkansas toothpicks" – were made locally and intended for use around the farm or ranch. As these weapons were virtually short swords – the blades could be up to a foot long – they were effective weapons for mounted raiders.

The Confederate Indians also brought their own horses with them to their unit. Many of the Indians in the Indian Territory were stockmen, especially those of the Choctaw and Chickasaw tribes. In 1861 and 1862 every enlistee either had a horse or could borrow one from friends or family.

As the war went on the Indians' herds disappeared, occasionally seized by Indians fighting for the other side. More often, whites from both Texas and Kansas confiscating "enemy property" appropriated them. Frequently the property had brands indicating that they belonged to Indians allied with the men that had seized them. Unless the owner was on hand to protest the seizure the horses would be adjudicated as enemy property. Confederate Indians resolved their shortage of mounts by using horses captured from the Union as remounts. Even when the Indians got paid, they were paid in money, not much-needed food or goods. While the Confederacy was more scrupulous about paying for goods requisitioned from Indians, it paid in Confederate banknotes – not specie.

Watcher McDonald was somewhat better equipped by the Union Army, which issued long-arms to their Indian soldiers. According to Wiley Britton, who served with the Indian Home Guard Regiments, the weapons varied by regiment. The 1st Indian Home Guard regiment was equipped with the US Army 1817 rifled musket. These had originally been flintlock weapons, but had been converted to use percussion caps. These weapons were so old that they used a spherical bullet. Indians issued these rifles were also issued spherical bullet molds. Too long to be aimed accurately from horseback, these rifles were deadly at long ranges when used dismounted. As Britton stated, "the Indians generally preferred

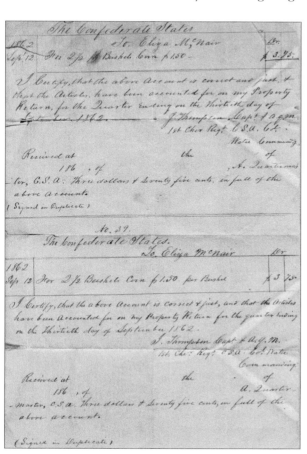

The Confederacy was scrupulous about paying their Indian allies fair value for supplies purchased, as evidenced by this receipt for fodder. Payment was made with Confederate banknotes, worthless after the war, rather than specie. (Cherokee Heritage Center)

them to the army musket then in use, and when fighting in timber where they could get a rest for their rifles, they were not to be despised on account of being antiquated."

Soldiers in Watcher's 2nd Indian Home Guard received Prussian rifles and muskets. These were muzzle-loading muskets built for the Prussian Army in the 1830s and 1840s, which fired the conical minié ball standard to the Union Army. Prussia, converting its army to breech-loading needle-guns in the early 1860s, sold tens of thousands of their surplus muzzle-loaders to both the Union and the Confederacy.

These weapons ranged from fair to awful. Some of those issued to the 2nd Indian Home Guard had been built as rifles, and were reasonable weapons. Others were smoothbore guns that had been converted to rifles by cutting grooves inside the barrel. They were acceptable, although less accurate than the purpose-built rifles. Others were unconverted smoothbores – short-range weapons in a campaign where long-range aimed fire was important. All had been converted from flintlock weapons to guns that used percussion caps.

The 3rd Indian Home Guard Regiment was issued a mix of Mississippi rifles and Prussian rifles. The Mississippi rifle was an excellent weapon that had been developed for use by the United States Army in 1841. While they had been superceded by the 1859 Harper's Ferry rifle, they were better than many of the weapons used by the Union's white regiments. They, too, used a minié ball. They were probably issued to the Indians because nothing worse remained in the armories when the 3rd Home Guard Regiment was raised in July 1862.

Along with the rifle, the Union Indians were given a cartridge box, in which to store their ammunition, which was plentiful. Yankee generosity ended with the rifle, cartridge box, and ammunition, however. No other equipment was issued to the Indian Brigade until later in the war.

The Union Army organized the Indian Home Guard regiments as infantry units, and the soldiers were paid at the lower rates of the infantryman. The Union recognized the value of mounted Indian soldiers, and the men that enlisted were permitted to bring their own horses and encouraged to ride them. This gave Union forces in the Indian Territory the effective equivalent of three additional cavalry regiments for the price of infantry units.

Initially, virtually all Union Indians were mounted. Like Watcher, they brought their own horses or borrowed mounts from friends or relatives who had spares. In 1861 the Northern Indians owned extensive herds of horses and cattle. They brought some with them to Kansas. Following the First Indian Expedition, they were able to recover some of the herds they had been forced to abandon in their flight.

As the war dragged on, their mounts became casualties and remounts became hard to find. White drovers were stealing Indians' herds, selling the horses to the Union Army to mount white cavalry units. An increasing number of Home Guard Indians – especially those from the Indian Territory – had to fight on foot. By 1864 virtually all members of the Home Guard units were dismounted. Since ultimate victory was apparent, the Union felt no urgent need to remount the Indian regiments, despite pleas from its commander, William Phillips.

The war would be won elsewhere. Except for the Indians that lived there (who could not vote, and therefore did not much matter), no one else cared about what happened in the Indian Territory.

IN THE ARMY: CONDITIONS OF SERVICE

When in garrison and not on campaign both George and Watcher lived in one of the Indian Territory's numerous "forts." The forts of the Indian Territory were more logistics centers than fortifications. The United States Army had erected most for the purpose of housing soldiers rather than defending territory. Several of the most important posts in and around the Indian Territory – Fort Scott, Fort Gibson, Fort Towson, and Fort Washita, among them – lacked palisades at the beginning of the Civil War.

Several "forts" – Coffee, Gibson, and Towson among them – were abandoned by the United States Army prior to the Civil War and turned over to the Indian Nation on which the land stood. In 1861 Fort Coffee was a boy's academy for the Chickasaw Nation, Fort Towson was the capitol building of the Choctaw Nation, and Fort Gibson a civilian town in the Cherokee Nation, briefly renamed Keetoowah.

Others, such as Forts Arbuckle, Cobb, and Washita, were used to run Indian Agencies that supplied tribes with Federal provisions, or held garrisons that protected the Five Civilized Tribes from the incursions of the more primitive Plains Indians. These forts, abandoned by their Union garrisons in May 1861, were quickly reoccupied by both Texas and Confederate Indian troops.

These collections of permanent buildings were about the only places where supplies could be safely stored, troops assembled and housed, and administrative functions performed. Fort Gibson housed the brigade in which George Campbell served until its capture by the Union in 1863. Thereafter it served as the focus of Union activities in the Indian Territory. Later in the war George Campbell and his regiment lived at Fort Coffee for part of the time, in barracks that in peacetime

A major source of food for the armies in the Indian Territory was beef from the herds that the Indians had run on their lands. Cattle belonging to enemy Indians were fair game. Cattle belonging to allied Indians had to be paid for. However, if you dressed the beef in the field – as shown here – embarrassing brands showing that allied Indians owned it disappeared. (Potter Collection)

had been the dormitory for the boys that attended the boarding school that it had become.

Besides Fort Gibson, the Mackay Salt Works was the main post for the Union Army in the Indian Territory. It was then one of the main local sources of salt, which was critical for preserving food. East of Fort Gibson, and north of the Arkansas River, it housed the 2nd Indian Home Guard Regiment to which Watcher belonged from 1863 through to the end of the war.

The value of Fort Gibson lay in its buildings, like this one. The Commissary Building, built in 1845, sheltered the supplies that an army needed for its continued existence. (Library of Congress, Prints and Photographs Division)

Garrison life

Garrison life was an ordeal for Indian soldiers. It was dull. At Mackay Salt Works Watcher mounted guard. He tended his gear and animals. Rather than barracks or cabins, Watcher, and the soldiers of the 2nd Home Guard, slept in army tents. Since they were there more or less permanently, they stockaded the sides of the tents with walls of split logs, and put in a wooden floor of split logs, which reduced the mud in the tents, and kept them warmer in the cold winter months.

The only distractions were ball games: a version of what would become lacrosse was played as avidly by members of the Civilized Tribes as baseball would be played by GIs during World War II. The ball-and-stick games began as part of the Indians' religion, but by the 1860s were played for secular amusement more than as religious ritual. The decline of a religious aspect did not reduce Indians' pursuit of this sport. They participated with a passion similar to the grip that high school football exerts today in small-town Texas and Oklahoma.

Nor was interest limited to Indians. When the Union Indians were in Kansas these games became a spectator event for nearby whites, both civilian and military. William Coffin, a Kansas Indian Agent, described one game in Kansas, where he watched "one hundred men stripped stark naked, except for a breech clout, the most athletic, muscular and powerful men, too, that I ever looked upon all exerting themselves to the utmost stretch of human exertion, with the wildest and most exciting shouts of triumph, defiance and determination."

Mostly though, you waited. "Hurry up and wait" was never a desirable state for a frontiersman, whether Indian or white, yet garrison duty was mostly that. Indian troops either became demoralized or deserted between battles.

The 2nd Home Guard lost nearly half its strength in July 1862 after capturing Fort Gibson, and settling in for less than a month of garrison duty. The Osage Indians in that regiment – 180 of them – left to go buffalo hunting. Many of the full-blooded Cherokees, those that were members of the Kee-too-wah Society, decided that the US Army was too slow a means of punishing the Confederate Cherokees. Scores left to seek private revenge against those that had driven them off their lands.

Others left to check on their farms and ranches. They had joined the army to recover their homesteads, and felt that while there was no active fighting, they should be free to put things to right at their homes. They planned to return when they had restored their farms.

This constant turnover of soldiers occurred in units on both sides of the conflict. The Union's 1st Indian Home Guard never counted more than 800 men on any one day of the Civil War, yet 3,274 Indians enlisted in the regiment between May 1862 and May 1865. The Confederate 1st Choctaw and Chickasaw Regiment – the first Indian Regiment raised and the longest-lived unit – was lucky to muster 800 men on

a good day, and probably fielded less than 250 on an average day. Yet 2,470 different men enlisted in the regiment over its lifetime.

Some of the turnover was due to casualties, but most was due to individual soldiers taking a casual view of enlistment. The three Union Indian regiments enrolled 8,003 different individuals during their existence. 1,018 Indians died while serving in these units, but only 2,400 men were present when the regiments mustered out in May 1865. The remaining 4,600 members simply disappeared. In December 1863, Cooper's Brigade – which included the 1st Choctaw and Chickasaw Regiment – had only 659 men present out of the 6,244 names listed on the muster rolls.

The sport of the Civilized Nations was a ball and stick game that developed into the modern game of lacrosse. This Catlain painting shows a ball game that took place near Fort Gibson, prior to the Civil War. (Library of Congress, Prints and Photographs Division)

Feuds

Turnover diminished as the war progressed. In many cases soldiers stayed with their units because their farms and ranches had ceased to exist. Indians' involvement in the Civil War resulted in civil wars within tribes. The Cherokee, Creek, and Seminole tribes each split into pro-Union and pro-Confederate factions, which coalesced into two formal governments for each of these tribes. Each faction believed it represented their tribe's legitimate government and that the other government stood for that tribe's traitors and turncoats.

Extremists on both sides destroyed private property belonging to those in the other faction. When the Union Army evacuated the Indian Territory in August 1862, Cherokee Principal Chief John Ross and other Cherokees who abjured the Confederate alliance and declared for the Union, joined the retreating Northern army. Rose Cottage – Ross's substantial three-story mansion in Park Hill – was burned to the ground after Confederate Cherokees reoccupied Park Hill, along with many other homes owned by Union Cherokees. Watcher's cabin was among them.

When the Union retook Park Hill in 1863, homes owned by Confederate Cherokees were torched. The damage was deliberate and planned. The few buildings standing in Park Hill by the end of the war were those owned by whites – the Indian Agents who chose to live with the Cherokee aristocracy, who stood outside the tribal feuds.

The process was repeated throughout the Indian Territory. Initially arsonists were individual Indians angered by others in their tribe who they regarded as traitors. The destruction grew until few private buildings remained standing between the Kansas border and the Red River. Destroying a rival's property was encouraged by a quirk of Indian

law. Indians did not own the land that their property sat upon – only the buildings and improvements. After George Campbell's Union neighbors burned down his family's plantation, they could have then gone before the Union Cherokee government to ask that the Campbell land be re-allotted to them as it was now "unimproved."

How much arson was motivated by greed and how much by hate is hard to say. The seeds of the civil wars within the Indian Nations went back for decades, even prior to removal to the Indian Territory. The anger felt by both sides went much deeper than the simple issues of whether one favored the Confederacy or the Union.

The loss of civilian housing reduced Indians of both sides to dependency upon the military for food and shelter. Wealthy Confederate Indians, like the Campbells, moved their families to northern Texas, along a strip in Choctaw and Chickasaw territory near the Red River. Wealthy Union Indians were denied even that much sanctuary as the guerrilla fighting in Kansas and Missouri made the northern border regions unsafe. All they could do was stay near military posts in Kansas and the Indian Territory with their poorer tribesmen.

Rations and supplies

Supply dominated the lives of everyone in the region, from the commanding generals to the ordinary soldiers, like George and Watcher, and even the civilians in the area – their families and friends. For both George and Watcher life, even in garrison, meant hunger.

The food was boring, if usually regular – at least for the soldiers. In garrison Watcher got rations issued to a Union soldier. On good days this was 20oz of fresh beef, probably taken from a steer formerly owned by an Indian. Had Watcher been at Fort Gibson, with its bake ovens, he would have received 22oz of soft bread. Instead, he received the prescribed alternative: 1lb of hard bread (called hard tack). He might also get his daily share of dried beans – about 6oz, cooked – and 1lb of coffee once every two weeks.

This provided 3,000 calories per day, which was enough for an active man. Often, the garrison had to go on short rations, as the Confederates frequently cut the supply lines. For their families and the other Indian civilians, both Confederate and Union, the inability to harvest crops or move sufficient food into the Indian Territory meant starvation. Years later, Mrs. C.B. Kagy recalled that her mother was one of the civilian Indians living around Fort Gibson during the Civil War: "Citizens had nothing more than bread [provided by Fort Gibson] and wild onions fried in tallow to eat." Soldiers with families would pass part of their ration to parents, wives, or children if they were living nearby.

George should have received the same rations as Watcher – the Confederacy used the same scale as the Union – but supply to the Indian Territory was unreliable. Most of George's food came from local sources, as long as there were some. His meals had greater variety if less certainty than Watcher's. Corn pone was frequently substituted for bread, and fresh pork for fresh beef. Or else they would eat Union rations captured during raids on supply trains.

The Indians were permitted to inhabit the Indian Territory partly because it was out of the way and hard to reach. There were no railroads. Steamboats only reached the periphery of the lands ceded to the Indians. Fort Gibson could only be reached by steamboat in late spring and early summer, when the water level was highest. Fort Smith, on the Arkansas border, was normally the head of navigation for the Arkansas River. The Red River, the boundary between Texas and the Indian Territory, could be reliably navigated as far west as Fort Towson.

The portions of the Indian Territory occupied by the Five Civilized Tribes was civilized by 19th-century standards. Yet this was still a frontier colony, dependent upon imports for the maintenance of civilization. The Campbell family grew their own food, producing a surplus for export. They spun their own cloth from cotton they raised, and they purchased leather goods from neighbors. Their tools, however, were imported. Everything from the paper for the local printing presses, to the engine parts that ran Indian-owned steamboats came from elsewhere. Watcher McDonald, as a fur trapper and subsistence farmer, depended upon imports for his gunpowder, traps, and shot.

From Fort Smith on the southeastern corner of the Choctaw Nation, goods had to be moved by wagon or pack train. It was 150 miles from the Red River to Fort Gibson, and roughly 75 miles from Fort Smith to Fort Gibson. It was 160 miles from Fort Washita to Fort Gibson, and 80 miles from Fort Washita to Fort Towson.

Reaching Fort Gibson from Fort Scott, Kansas required an overland trek of 175 miles. Fort Scott could not be reached by steamboat or railroad during the Civil War. Goods that reached Fort Gibson from Fort

Civil War supply lines to the Indian Territory.

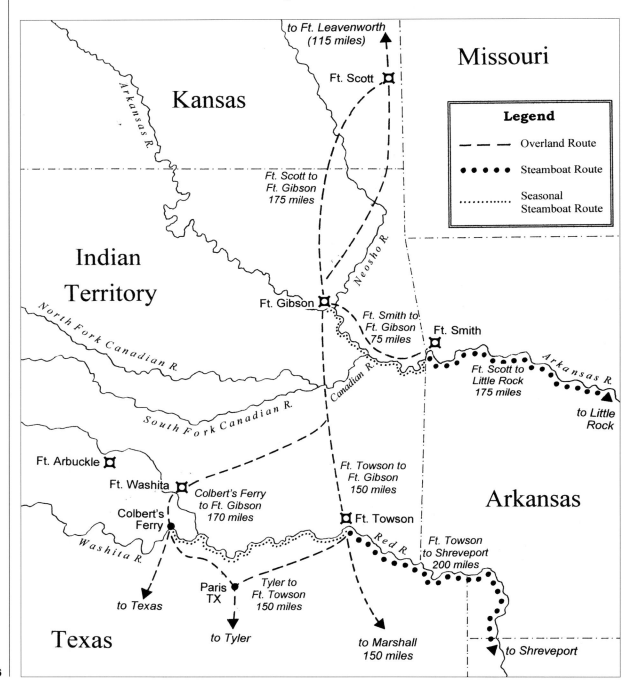

Scott first had to travel overland an additional 115 miles from Fort Leavenworth, Kansas, or via Independence, Missouri, to reach Fort Scott. Under normal circumstances it could take a wagon two weeks to travel from the Missouri River to Fort Gibson.

In peacetime a wagonload or two of manufactured goods – including powder and shot – met the demands of a farming community for a year. But the war strained transportation networks throughout the United States, as both sides geared up for a war economy. The Indians were totally dependent upon what was shipped to them – and little got through. Richmond's orders to supply the Indians were ignored by the surrounding states until the needs of their own units were satisfied.

Soon other factors choked the flow of goods to the Indian Territory. The Unionists captured the Mississippi watershed, cutting steamboat traffic. New Orleans' fall in April 1862 severed the Indian Territory's only water route to the outside world. The Union took Memphis, Tennessee, in June 1862, eliminating the Indians' access to Tennessee's manufacturing center. Little Rock, Arkansas, fell in 1863, further isolating the Indian Territory from the South.

By 1863 it was impossible to grow crops in the Creek and Cherokee Nations. By then, George's family had fled to Texas. The Indians' herds of cattle and horses were disappearing, gathered by whites from Texas and Kansas to meet both armies' need for food and mounts. It took an overland journey of 150 miles to reach Marshall, Texas, or Tyler, Texas – the two northernmost Texas towns manufacturing military goods. These towns were 200 miles from ports on the Texas coast.

In 1864 the war moved into the Choctaw and Chickasaw Nations, making it impossible to raise food anywhere in the Five Civilized Nations. All foodstuffs had to be imported – enough to feed the civilian population as well as military personnel.

Both sides became reliant upon supply trains. Watcher helped guard trains against the raids of the Confederates. Every piece of clothing or ammunition issued to Watcher started from Fort Leavenworth and followed a long road to Fort Gibson. Food such as grain, flour, or beef could be gathered around Fort Scott, and only had to move 175 miles. The bake ovens at Fort Scott and Fort Gibson were feeding most of the Union Indian soldiers and their families that were in the Indian Territory by the start of 1864.

The oxen and horses pulling the wagons had to be fed. The land between Fort Scott and Fort Gibson was a natural hayfield, but what was a simple task in peacetime became a challenge during the war. Hay-gathering parties became targets, and requiring armed escorts. George once helped set the prairie north of the Verdigris River on fire to burn the hay before Union forces could gather it.

Without railroads or steamboats, supplies – both Union and Confederate – had to be transported by wagons once past the boundaries of the Indian Territory. The limitation of draft animals meant that both sides could supply troops only as far as Fort Gibson. (Potter Collection)

In the face of such opposition, supply trains brought only a minimum of the supplies required to keep the Union garrisons in Fort Gibson clothed, armed, and fed – with barely enough extra food to keep Indian civilians from starving. Many died – leaving Watcher grateful that he was an orphan, without the responsibilities that so many of his comrades had of keeping their families fed.

ON CAMPAIGN

For Indians like George Campbell and Watcher McDonald life on campaign was similar to life in garrison. There were differences: meals were more uncertain on campaign and living conditions were primitive, at least by the standards of the Civilized Indians. They spent more time walking and less time riding than they would have preferred. Medical services were inconsistent and field sanitation barely adequate. Units typically marched too quickly for the soldiers to appreciate the country through which they were traveling – assuming that they had the energy to play tourist, and were not exhausted from too much marching and not enough food. Then, too, there was the danger of being shot at, frequently, and when the soldiers least expected it.

Indians of the Civilized Nations generally liked the outdoors. The typical Indian of the Civilized Nations could live outdoors as well as his white counterparts in Texas and Kansas. Most enjoyed hunting and fishing. Ranching – with the attendant drives and herding activities – was a preferred way for a Choctaw or Chickasaw to earn a living. But these Indians were homebodies, not plains nomads. In May 1863 Cherokee Jason Bell, a captain in Stand Watie's regiment, wrote in a letter home, "How I would like to settle down again and hear the cows lowing, the hogs squealing, and the yard with roses in it, the waving wheat and the stately corn growing..." For men like him, the best way to finish a day spent enjoying the outdoors was in bed at home. Even a barracks beat a night in the open air, especially when the nights were wet or cold.

The magazine at Fort Gibson, built in 1845, provided one of the few secure places to store large quantities of gunpowder in the Indian Territory. Prior to Fort Gibson's capture by the North, it gave the Confederates a place to refresh their ammunition, which in turn was a major reason for the Confederate victory against Opothleyohola's loyalists. By the third battle with the Confederates, the loyalists were out of gunpowder, while the Confederate troops had plenty. (Library of Congress, Prints and Photographs Division)

By the fall of 1861 nearly 2,500 Indians were in Confederate regiments. Virtually every Indian unit raised by the Confederacy was a mounted rifle force. Towards the end of the Civil War, the Chickasaw Nation, fearing a shortage of horses, raised an infantry regiment, but this was quickly altered to a mounted unit. The three Indian Home Guard Regiments raised by the Union were organized and paid as infantry regiments, but until they ran out of horses, they fought as mounted rifles.

In the early 19th century mounted rifles filled a niche between cavalry and infantry. Like dragoons, they were intended to fight both mounted or on foot. While dragoons were traditionally armed with smoothbore muskets or musketoons, mounted infantry used a rifled firearm, frequently a carbine. Since a rifle had a much longer range than a smoothbore, mounted rifles were used as skirmishers, who scouted ahead of a main body, then deployed into a skirmish line – dismounted if the terrains supported it – that both fixed the enemy and denied it information about the force opposing them.

The rifled musket, which gave soldiers the range of a rifleman with the rate of fire available to musketeers, eliminated much of the uniqueness of the mounted rifleman. By the Civil War most cavalry were in fact, if not in name, mounted rifles, and fought dismounted when circumstances dictated.

Opothleyohola's force

The only overtly loyalist forces were those of Opothleyohola, an Upper Creek chief and, ironically, a slave owner. In his youth he had fought the United States during the War of 1812. That war cemented his loyalty to the United States – or at very least gave him an appreciation for the capabilities of the Federal troops that younger and rasher Indian leaders lacked. He led the Creek faction that opposed union with the Confederacy.

His stand attracted other loyalist Indians – not just Creeks, but also Seminoles and Cherokees – as well as escaping slaves. By the fall of 1861 perhaps 6,000 other loyalist Indians and escaping slaves had gathered around him. Most were women, children, and old men. Opothleyohola appealed to the Federal government in Kansas for aid, but by October, the loyalists realized that the Union was not coming. A Confederate column, consisting of troops from Texas, the Confederate Creeks, and the Choctaw and Chickasaw Regiment commanded by Col. Douglas Cooper, was approaching, so Opothleyohola ordered his people to Kansas.

The loyalist column had 300 runaway slaves and 1,200 Seminole and Creek fighting men – including young boys and old men – for protection. A lack of weapons, limited stores of ammunition, and poor organization handicapped the loyalists. The runaway slaves had neither firearms nor the training to use weapons. Many of the Indian warriors were older men. Few were armed with more than hunting rifles, and they only had enough powder and shot for peacetime hunting. Additionally, the loyalists lacked organization. They came as individuals dissatisfied with the decisions of their various tribes to ally with the Confederacy.

The loyalists fled as families, carrying what possessions they could in wagons and on pack animals. Many brought their livestock with them. The column crawled north and east, a combination of wagon train and trail drive.

The Confederate forces soon caught Opothleyohola's people. In three battles fought from late November until the end of December 1861, Cooper's Texas and Indian forces destroyed the loyalist column. While some Texan forces participated – mainly irregular cavalry – the Opothleyohola campaign primarily pitted Indian against Indian. Formal Indian military units organized in European fashion fought against traditional Indian war bands. The European model emerged victorious.

Two Creek regiments, a Choctaw and Chickasaw regiment, and Stand Watie's Cherokee regiment – made up of Indians that had assimilated European ways, including George Campbell – enthusiastically assaulted their loyalist kinsmen. A second Cherokee regiment, Drew's Mounted Rifles, which was made up of traditionalist Cherokees – balked. As Albert Pike, the former Indian Agent who then commanded the Confederate Indians, wrote, these men "did not wish to fight their brethren, the Creeks." Many deserted rather than fight other Indians. Some joined Opothleyohola before the battle of Chusto-talasah.

During this winter campaign, it was harder for the loyalists than the Confederates. The loyalists depended on food

As a young man Opothleyohola fought against the United States during the War of 1812. In his sixties at the outset of the Civil War, he was convinced that the United States would defeat the Confederacy as it had the "Red Sticks." His refusal to side with the Confederacy thrust him into leadership of the loyalist faction. (Western History Collections, University of Oklahoma Library)

and shelter that they brought with them. After Chusto-talasah and Chustenahalan they were reduced to what they could carry. George and his compatriots could get food and clothing from their bases. The cold weather made travel difficult, even for the better-supplied Confederates. A heavy snowfall the day after Chustenahalan deterred the Confederate pursuit of the scattered loyalists. The Confederates returned to warm barracks, as the destitute loyalist survivors trickled into Kansas over the next month.

Confederate Indian units were raised for local defense, and by the terms of their treaty they were to remain within the Indian Territory. Yet there were times that the Confederate Indian regiments were called out of the Indian Territory. The first was during the Pea Ridge campaign in the spring of 1862. Later, Confederate Indian units fought at battles in Newtonia in late 1863 and at Poison Springs, Arkansas, in 1864.

The reactions of the various Indian regiments to these deployments varied according to the personalities of the commanders and the sentiments of the men. At Pea Ridge, most of the Indian units – two Creek regiments (which included an attached Seminole battalion) and the Choctaw and Chickasaw regiment – refused to move, citing a lack of pay. Even after their back pay was received, most of the units moved slowly, unwilling to leave the Indian Territory. Only part of one Creek

regiment willingly left the Indian Territory for Arkansas. The two Cherokee units – one regiment commanded by Stand Watie, and another by John Drew – went to Arkansas. Having fought at Wilson's Creek, Watie's unit was eager to go. Drew's men were more reluctant. Apart from participating in a cavalry charge on the first day of battle, they proved unenthusiastic about fighting outside their home region.

This reluctance was motivated, in part, because the Indians regarded Pea Ridge as an attempt to acquire land outside the Indian Territory. It might help the South strategically, but the Indians tended to view it as an attempt to lure them into a war in which they had no interest.

At Newtonia and Poison Springs the pattern was different. Both of those battles were fought to blunt Union drives into the Indian Territory through western Arkansas. The Union had invaded the Indian Territory once by the time Newtonia was fought, and although they had withdrawn, the Indians participated at Newtonia in the spirit that the best place to defend your home was in a back yard other than your own. Similarly, at Poison Springs, the Choctaws and Chickasaw were trying to protect the Red River valley from Union invasion.

The Union Indians were more willing to fight outside the Indian Territory. They started their war in Kansas, and had begged to be permitted to fight. "We had not come here to live at the expense of the government," Opothleyohola appealed. "Send to us ammunition and transportation as early as possible – we ask no more." When the Federal government finally raised Indian regiments, they fought wherever they were asked to fight. They preferred fighting in the Indian Territory, but through most of 1862 and early 1863 they were forced to fight outside it, until the Union finally secured Fort Gibson.

Initially, conditions for the two first Union Indian regiments were primitive. They set out from Kansas with no regimental baggage. They lacked tents, cooking pots, and other regimental equipment. They had no surgeons or medical supplies, and were dependent upon the accompanying white regiments for medical care. Watcher spent his nights sleeping under the stars or, when time permitted, in a brush lean-to assembled at the end of the day. His meals on this campaign were equally Spartan. He received biscuit – hard tack – and a piece of raw

In the field, food would have been weighed out and issued to individual soldiers in a manner such as shown in this illustration. (Potter Collection)

beef, which he had to cook on a stick over a campfire. By Newtonia in October 1862, the Union Indians had acquired both tents and cooking pots. While conditions improved over the course of the war, the Union Indians seemed to be perpetually at the end of the supply line.

It took two attempts for the Union armies to anchor themselves in the Indian Territory. The First Indian Expedition captured Fort Gibson, and caused the defection of Drew's Mounted Rifles to the Union, but a pusillanimous withdrawal of white troops by an incompetent commander forced the retreat of the Indian regiments as well. It was not until the spring of 1863 that the Union reestablished itself – this time permanently – in Fort Gibson.

When the Union Army moved south of Fort Gibson in July 1863 the Confederates seized the opportunity to attack the Yankees outside the protection of the fort. Concentrating their forces, the Confederates outnumbered the Northern army nearly two to one.

They struck the Union Army as they were crossing Honey Creek on July 17, 1863. The Confederates overheard an order for Union cavalry, scouting ahead, to fall back. Assuming it was a general order, the Southern cavalry charged into the Union center, anchored by the waiting black troops, lying on the ground. They stood, fired, and demolished the Confederate center. The Indian regiments on the flanks finished the job started by the blacks, destroying the Confederate Army, their last major field force in the Indian Territory.

Honey Springs irrevocably changed the balance of power in the Indian Territory, demolishing Confederate ability to meet the Union Army in the field. The fall of Little Rock, in September 1863, finally allowed the resupply of Fort Gibson by river.

A: Private, Union Indian Brigade, 1862

B: Recruiting

B

C: Outfitting the Indian soldier – the Trans-Missisppi Way

D: The battle of Chustenahalan, December 26, 1861

E: Fort Gibson, June 1863

E

F: Raid on a hay party, 1864

Homecoming, 1865

H: Sergeant, Cherokee 1st Mounted Rifles, 1864

The North failed to exploit its advantages, content to maintain what they already held. Neither Union nor Confederate Indians had enough resources to control the entire Indian Territory alone. The Union and the Confederacy refused to commit more white troops to the region, using their manpower in other theaters. For two years, the region was frequently raided ground.

Stand Watie's raids

The Confederates, led by Stand Watie, proved adept at guerrilla tactics. They attacked supply trains, or parties sent to gather hay, and isolated groups of patrolling Union soldiers. The Union forces responded in kind, launching raids into the southern half of the Indian Territory. When Lincoln issued his Proclamation of Amnesty in December 1863, William Phillips, then commanding the Union Indian Brigade, had translations printed in different Indian languages. He distributed the proclamations during a raid in the Choctaw Nation, with a message: accept amnesty or be destroyed. While this action undermined Lincoln's intention, it reflected the attitude of many of the Indians serving under Phillips.

The exploits of Stand Watie and his Confederate Indians were brilliant and militarily glorious, but strategically sterile. The Confederates could not loosen the Union grip on Fort Gibson. Two years of raids and counter-raids reduced most buildings in the Indian Territory to burnt ruins. At the war's end, most of the Indian families – both Confederate and Union – lived as refugees, near Fort Gibson, at the fringes of the Indian Territory or the surrounding states.

The destruction was carried out by Indians, against Indians. The whites did not really care about the Indian Territory. The Confederacy wooed the Indian Nations as a way to protect an exposed northwestern flank. As the Confederacy staggered under the hammer blows of the Union armies, the Confederate states became less interested in the Trans-Mississippi region. The Union intervened to ease a refugee problem. As long as the North held Fort Gibson, most of the Indian refugees remained in the Indian Territory, not Kansas. But the internal

The battle of Honey Springs gave the Union dominance in the Indian Territory. The Union failure to reinforce this victory condemned the Indian Territory to two years of bloody stalemate. (Potter Collection)

tribal passions released by the American Civil War consumed the Indian Territory like a prairie fire, as the actions of one side led to reprisals that spurred yet more retaliation in turn.

Injury and capture

The Indian Territory was a bad place to get injured. Civil War-era military medicine was poor, even at its best, and in the Indian Territory, it was far from its best. A battlefield injury would be treated in an open aid station, set up in a field, more often than not. Field surgery consisted mainly of amputating limbs shattered by bullets.

This assumed the fight where the injury occurred was large enough to merit a surgeon in the field. Most of the combat in the Indian Territory consisted of small raids and patrols. Typically, only a company or two would be involved. Surgeons generally stayed in the garrison unless the entire regiment was committed to battle. An injured man might go hours – possibly days if injured during a deep raid – before receiving any medical attention other than what his comrades could give him on the spot.

Once he got back to garrison – if severely injured – his troubles were only just beginning. Hospital facilities were inadequate – even by Civil War standards. There were no hospitals in the Indian Territory before the Civil War. During the Civil War both sides used public buildings such as schools or churches as hospitals. Schools were a better option as most of the schools in the Indian Territory were boarding schools, with both beds and kitchen facilities. While they could draw upon the doctors and surgeons in the area to provide basic medical services, they lacked nursing staff.

If you were lucky, a family member would look after you. When George Washington Grayson, a lieutenant in the Creek 2nd Mounted Rifle Regiment contracted smallpox, he survived only because his mother came to the hospital where he was being kept and stayed with him to tend to his needs until he recovered.

Combat injuries were not the major cause of death among the soldiers of either side: disease was the real killer. Of the 1,018 Indians

The Chickasaw Rock Academy was one of the public schools in the Indian Territory. During the Civil War, the school was closed and the academy was used first as a barracks and then as a hospital. (Western History Collections, University of Oklahoma Library)

who died while enrolled in the Union Army, 775 – three-quarters – died from disease. Only 107 were killed on the battlefield or died of wounds received in battle.

Being taken prisoner was chancier than avoiding injury on the battlefield. Confederate Indians rarely took Union Indians prisoner. Watcher's chance of being taken prisoner was better than the Kee-too-wah members that fought the Confederates outside the structure of the Union Army. These free agents were termed "Pins" or "Shucks" (see page 48) by the Confederates, and were shot out of hand if caught.

If Watcher were to be captured he might be treated as a prisoner of war – if his captors belonged to organized Confederate units and not one of the many irregular bands such as Quantrell's marauding the Trans-Mississippi. Watcher's chances were better if a white unit from Texas or Arkansas were the captors because they had less emotional investment in the war in the Indian Territory. Many of the soldiers in the Indian Regiment viewed the Union Indians as traitors, even those in organized regiments, and disposed of them on the spot.

Should a Union Indian be taken prisoner, a bleak fate awaited him. He would be sent to a prison camp at Tyler or Marshall, Texas. While the Texas camps lacked the cruelty of Andersonville, life in them was hard. They were overcrowded, and Confederate shortages of both food and clothing in northern Texas were felt most keenly by the inmates of those camps. They got what was left after everyone else.

Life was easier for captured Confederate Indians. Unless they were taken by white Jayhawkers from Kansas or the Indian guerrillas seeking personal revenge against the Confederate Indians, their surrender was likely to be accepted. Captured Confederate Indians were generally sent to the Union's prison camp at Alton, Illinois. The surgeon of Drew's Mounted Rifles was sent there after being captured at Pea Ridge.

Confederate Indians taken prisoner often ended up in the prisoner of war camp in Alton, Illinois, but some captured Choctaws ended up being sent to Fort Columbus in New York City, pictured here. (Library of Congress, Prints and Photographs Division)

The status of Confederate Indians taken prisoner was unique. Technically they were the only prisoners captured by the Union that were not in rebellion. They belonged to sovereign nations that had formally declared war on the United States. Possibly as a result of that, in May 1863 at least one group of Choctaw Indians was sent to Fort Columbus in New York harbor.

Conflict continued in the Indian Territory until the end of the Civil War – and beyond. Confederate forces west of the Mississippi were the last to get the word about the defeat of the Confederacy, and the last to disperse. Kirby-Smith, commander of the Trans-Mississippi District, never really surrendered, and simply sent his men home in May 1865. The Indian forces in the Indian Territory were the last Confederate forces to disperse, continuing resistance until June 1865 before surrendering.

For both George and Watcher, hardship did not end with the close of the Civil War. Both of their homes were in ashes. Confederate Cherokees had burned Watcher's small cabin after the First Indian Expedition withdrew from the Indian Territory in 1862. The plantation belonging to George Campbell's family, the home in which he had grown up, and in which he was living at the beginning of the war, met a similar fate in the winter of 1864. Members of the Union Indian Brigade destroyed every building after George's father refused to accept Lincoln's amnesty. By that time, George's family was living with distant Choctaw cousins near the Red River.

Rebuilding was complicated because the Indian Nations had formally declared war on the United States, and peace required them to

After the surrenders of Lee's and Hood's armies, the Confederacy still had an effective army in the Trans-Mississippi District, commanded by General Edmund Kirby-Smith. On May 26, 1865, Kirby-Smith (pictured here) sent his army home. This included all of the Indian regiments except for those commanded by Stand Watie at Doaksville. (Author's collection)

sign treaties that cost each nation land and money. Watcher's cabin could not be rebuilt because it was located on land the Cherokee Nation ceded to new tribes as part of the peace treaty the Cherokee Nation signed in 1866. As these new Indians came to the Indian Territory from the Great Lakes region, Watcher was forced to build a new home elsewhere if he wanted to remain in the Cherokee Nation.

The Campbells were more fortunate. They could rebuild in their old location. Even then, their task was daunting. They had lost all of their possessions, except for a wagonload that they had taken with them to the Red River. Their livestock was gone. The money and tools they had brought with them when they had relocated to the Indian Territory in the 1830s had been destroyed by the war. Since Mr. Campbell's slaves had been emancipated, they lacked a labor force – except family.

Unlike many Cherokees, Creeks, and Seminoles, the Campbells and McDonalds – or rather the sole McDonald, since Watcher had been orphaned in 1860, when both parents had died of disease – decided to put the war behind them, and work together. Watcher helped his cousins build their new homes, and George helped Watcher build a new cabin.

BELIEF AND BELONGING

Why did the Indians of the Indian Territory enlist to fight in the Civil War? The first wave joined for the glory and the adventure, or to defend their homeland. This group joined Confederate regiments. The next wave joined for revenge or to reclaim lost lands. Initially, this group consisted of Indians that joined the Union regiments. Eventually, as the tides of war in the Indian Territory shifted from the Confederates to the Union, revenge and reconquest became a major motivation for Indians joining Confederate units. Finally, Indians ended up enlisting in the Indian regiments of both sides because they had no choice. Neutrality became impossible. Survival – for both the males of fighting age and their families – required a choice between the North or the South.

The Five Civilized Nations were in a period of flux at the start of the Civil War, in the process of adopting white customs, attitudes, and technology into their traditional ways of life. The transition was a rocky one, further complicated by a forced move to the Indian Territory, which some Indians opposed while others acquiesced. A large group – like George Campbell's immediate family – chose to assimilate white ways. These were often the Indians that had intermarried with whites or blacks. Others, including George's cousin Watcher McDonald, preferred the traditional ways. The Civil War focused these different approaches into open conflict, as a lens concentrates sunlight into flame.

The Choctaw and Chickasaw had almost completely assimilated into European lifestyles and the lives they led were little different from most frontier whites. The other three tribes still had large elements that wished to continue their lives in the manner of their fathers and grandfathers, as small-holding farmers raising enough to feed their family with a small surplus to trade for the necessities that they could not produce themselves such as manufactured goods, gunpowder, and firearms. They saw plantation farming with chattel slavery and an emphasis on material acquisition as a threat to that lifestyle.

To the assimilationist Indians, the traditional Indians were the problem. It was the old story of the converted being the most fervent advocates of a position. They felt the traditional ways stood in the way of progress and acceptance by the United States. Acceptance of their tribe – whether Chickasaw, Choctaw, or Cherokee – as equals to the whites, not second-class or second-best, was important to them. One of the reasons the Confederate alliance was so seductive was that – on paper – the Confederacy offered equality. The Indian Nations were given voting representation in the Confederate assembly. The Confederacy offered to pay the Indians the relocation monies still owed by the Federal government.

Trade routes flowed to New Orleans, linking the Civilized Tribes economically to the Confederacy. The plantation aristocracy that ran the politics of the tribes was also emotionally linked to the Old South. After the Union defeat at Bull Run, followed by the Confederate victory at Wilson's Creek – a battlefield in Missouri so close to the Indian Territory that a battalion of Cherokees participated – establishment of the Confederacy seemed an accomplished fact. The promised prize was enough to lead the assimilated Indians – those that had adopted the whites' technologies and attitudes – to declare for the Confederacy.

The traditionalist Indians rejected this alliance for three major reasons. First, they did not want to become involved in white wars. When they had – during the War of 1812, and the Mexican–American War – things had deteriorated for the Indians, even those allied with the United States. Next, the citizens of the Confederate states were the ones whose demands had led to exile in the Indian Territory. The citizens of Georgia, Alabama, Tennessee, and Mississippi had forced them west of the Mississippi River. Texans and Arkansans had chased them out of those states.

Combined with news of Bull Run, the Union defeat at Wilson's Creek, Arkansas, in August 1861 convinced the Civilized Tribes that the Confederacy was going to win. It forced the Cherokee Nation to abandon neutrality and declare for the Confederacy, which cut off the loyal Creeks and Seminoles from Kansas. (Library of Congress, Prints and Photographs Division)

Finally, the United States government had a habit of winning wars, and punishing tribes that opposed them. Indians that had fought the United States – men like Opothleyohola and the Seminole chief Billy Bowlegs – tended to view the Confederacy as yet another tribe, albeit white, that was going to be crushed by the Federal government, just as the Creeks and Seminoles had.

The traditional Indians felt neutrality was the best course, but their assimilated cousins blocked that option. The Indian alliance with the Confederacy was made for political advantage, not survival. Forcing the traditionalists to choose sides turned it into a war for survival for the Indians opposed to the Confederacy, which in turn transformed the Civil War in the Indian Territory into a war to the knife, a total war.

Secret societies

The two major Indian secret societies, the Kee-too-wah and the Knights of the Golden Circle, reflected the cultural divide among the Indians.

A Baptist minister who was a full-blooded Cherokee organized the Kee-too-wah in 1859. Membership at that time was limited to full-blooded Cherokees. The mission of the Kee-too-wah society was to protect traditional Cherokee ways (as modified by Christianity) and defend the interests of the full-blooded members of the Cherokee Nation.

Members identified themselves by wearing crossed straight pins (or a single straight pin) on the left lapel or left breast of their hunting jackets. Alternatively, they would pin a corn shuck to their clothing or plait a shuck in their hair. In daylight, members greeted each other by drawing their left lapel forward and rightward across the heart when passing. In the dark, one member would issue a challenge saying "Tahlequah – who are you?" The proper response was, "I am Kee-too-wah's son!"

The society adopted the American flag as its emblem, underscoring an anti-secessionist attitude. The society became abolitionist early in its existence, viewing chattel slavery as incompatible with both Christianity and the traditional Cherokee way of life. As such, the society was tremendously threatening to the Cherokee propertied class. After the Cherokee Nation allied with the Confederacy, members of Kee-too-wah were viewed with suspicion, and many were driven out of the Indian Territory as Northern sympathizers.

While many members of the Kee-too-wah initially enlisted in the Indian Home Guard in 1862, many became impatient when the Northern government failed – in the members' eyes – to adequately punish Cherokees that supported secession. These Kee-too-wah members deserted the army to be free to take what they felt was appropriate action more directly. Along with abolitionist Jayhawkers from Kansas, they provided a Northern counterpoint to the terrorism conducted by Southern bushwackers. All of these groups contributed significantly to the brutality of the Civil War in the Western frontier.

The Knights of the Golden Circle were the Confederate counterpart to the Kee-too-wah. The Knights of the Golden Circle had its roots in the Masonic tradition. Founded in 1854 in Cincinnati, Ohio, it quickly spread south, with a significant number of lodges in Texas and Arkansas. By 1861 there were several chapters in the Indian Territory made up of mixed-blood Indians and local whites. Stand Watie was a Knight. So was

Albert Pike, the former Indian Agent from Arkansas who convinced the Indian Nations to join the Confederacy. At the time of the Civil War the Knights held a pro-slavery and, frankly, racist position.

While membership by Indians in an organization that espoused racial superiority may seem surprising, it underscores the degree to which the wealthy Indians thought themselves part of the planter aristocracy. The Choctaw Nation then had one of the most restrictive black codes in the United States. The Civilized Tribes began as warrior nations. The Cherokee and Choctaw were highly ethnocentric, believing themselves superior to all other peoples white, black or Indian.

Whites, by virtue of martial prowess were conceded to be equals, to be emulated. This was especially true of the planter aristocracy, whose views on warfare and class mirrored those of these Indians. But blacks were regarded as a servant class. From the first contact with people of the Old World, the Choctaw, Cherokee, and Chickasaw had seen the blacks as servile laborers, inferiors that were incapable of being warriors.

The situation was more complicated among the Creeks, and especially the Seminoles (who had intermarried with runaway slaves to form a new tribe), but these nations were viewed as the more backward of the five. Additionally, the Seminole was both the smallest of the Five Civilized Nations, and the last to find a place in the Indian Territory.

The Indian members of the Knights of the Golden Circle were equally contemptuous of their full-blooded cousins, dehumanizing them by calling them "Pins" or "Shucks" (from the emblems of the Kee-too-wah).

At the battle of Honey Springs the Confederate Indians attacked, despite having damp gunpowder. Having discovered that their opponents had a black regiment, they believed that "niggers" would not fight, and the "Shucks" would fight poorly. The Confederates, both Indian and white Texans, wanted to force a battle before the blacks ran away. Instead, the blacks waited, held their line, and blasted the Confederate cavalry charge apart with disciplined rifle fire.

Yet anti-black sentiment was never far from the surface of the Confederate Indians. White soldiers were permitted to surrender, but after Honey Springs this was a nicety denied to black soldiers, who were usually killed out of hand. Sometimes a Confederate victory concluded with a hunt for surviving black soldiers.

Religion

By 1861 most of the Indians in the Civilized Tribes were Christian. The conversion was sincere and by the end of the 1850s there were enough Indian ministers that the missionary societies were withdrawing their missions because these Indians were no longer viewed as a heathen people. Even the two principal Indian secret societies, the Knights of the Golden Circle and the Kee-too-wah, were based on Christian foundations. The individual nations built churches for their communities, and missionaries were running most Indian schools. Christianity was at the center of the Indians' society, and a major motivation in their activities.

Some Indians, especially traditionalists, still maintained the old religions. Each tribe had a traditional religion that was animist in nature. They shared characteristics: they believed in a creator, or Great Spirit; they attempted to put the believers in harmony with the world through a variety of rites, ceremonies, and actions, and explained natural phenomena by anthropomorphizing them. For example, in the traditional Cherokee religion, the Sun and the Moon were sister and brother, and the animals arranged in tribes, just like humans.

Many of the activities associated with Indians in war, including wearing war paint, and holding a ceremonial dance before a battle, were called for by their traditional religion, and were religious in nature. Whether Christian or traditional believers, the Indian participants in the Civil War often fell back on the old beliefs in times of stress.

Before the First Indian Expedition started, soldiers in the two Indian Home Guard Regiments held the rituals prescribed by the old religious traditions. This involved consuming the black drink – a purgative that induced vomiting, and a night of ritual dancing, followed by a plunge in the river. The ritual was supposed to make the participant bulletproof.

While most of the Indians belonging to the Civilized Nations were Christian, some clung to the old traditions, partly out of belief, but mostly due to tradition. Before the First Indian Expedition left camp, members of the Indian regiments held a war dance. (Potter Collection)

With inadequate food, the inferior equipment issued to them, and the unenthusiastic attitude of the Union Army to these troops, even skeptical Indians probably felt that if the ceremony offered even a small advantage it was worth taking.

Nor were the more assimilated Southern Indians immune to the lure of such protections. George Washington Grayson related in his memoirs that members of his company had "great faith in certain Indian war medicines said to afford protection against the casualties of battle." Grayson declined the offer of such a treatment, as he wanted to prove that he was courageous enough to take part in battle without such protection.

WAR ON THE PLAINS: EXPERIENCE OF BATTLE

The Indians of the Civilized Nations, like their frontier white counterparts, were first-rate fighters, but untrained soldiers. They knew how to hunt and shoot, and used these peacetime skills in combat. Their battles resembled large-scale hunting parties, with other humans as quarry, and the quarry fighting back.

The three battles fought in the Opothleyohola campaign of 1861 illustrate this best. Fought between traditionalist Indians loyal to the United States and Confederate Indians with the assistance of two regiments of Texas frontiersmen who were culturally similar to their Indian allies, the tactics used by both sides were those familiar to hunters.

The Union Indians set up ambushes in strongpoints that were functionally similar to duck blinds or deer stands used in Texas and Oklahoma today. They hid the rifleman from his quarry – in this case the Confederate troops – and also provided protection against enemy fire. The Confederates set up skirmish lines that moved forward like a line of drivers, beating the ground to flush their quarry – the Union loyalists.

Opothleyohola's campaigns

At Round Mountain in November 1861, Texas cavalry met sentries from Opothleyohola's force. When the Texas company, some 40 men, charged, the Indians fell back, disappearing into timber lining Walnut Creek, near the Red Fork of the Arkansas River. When the Texans pursued, other Indians, hidden in the wood, opened fire, driving the Texans back. The Union Indians chased these scouts until both scouts and the Union Indians reached the main Confederate force. Both sides fought dismounted, lying or kneeling as cover afforded.

A Seneca Indian, Ely Parker became the highest-ranking Indian in the Union Army during the Civil War. An engineering officer, he was on General Grant's staff in 1865, when this photograph was taken. After the war he became a general, and President Grant's Commissioner of the Bureau of Indian Affairs. (Library of Congress, Prints and Photographs Division)

The Union Indians began flanking the Confederates, moving through cover like hunters stalking prey. While the Confederates with roughly 1,400 men – mostly Creeks, Choctaws, and Chickasaws – probably outnumbered the Union forces, Douglas Cooper, commanding the Confederates, thought he was outnumbered and fell back. The battle continued until after dark, when the Union Indians – their families escaping during the battle – slipped away.

Casualties were light on both sides. This was the first Indian Territory battle of the war and like most inexperienced troops both sides shot high. Additionally, the targets for both sides were under cover.

The battle of Chusto-talasah (or Bird Creek) on December 9 followed the pattern of the first fight. The Union Indians fortified an encampment along Bird Creek, and a Confederate force of 2,000 of the Cherokee Drew's Mounted Rifles with an additional Texas cavalry regiment (the 4th Texas Cavalry) attacked.

The pro-Union forces fired from cover, while the Confederate center, led by the Creek regiment, dismounted and crawled forward until they were close enough to charge the Union works. In hand-to-hand fighting akin to traditional Indian warfare, the Confederate Creeks drove the Union Indians from the timber barricade on the Confederate left. Knives, tomahawks, and butted rifles decided the outcome.

While Texas cavalry covered the right, a 100-man company from the Choctaw and Chickasaw regiment charged on horseback to a cabin and corncrib anchoring the center of the Union line, dismounted and took the cabin. Once both sides had fired their rifles, that battle also became a hand-to-hand fight.

As before, the Confederates held the field, but the pro-Union Indians slipped away. Again, casualties were light on both sides, despite the fury, fewer than three dozen men in total were killed. Opothleyohola stated that nine of his force was killed. Cooper reported 15 dead and 37 wounded on his side.

Opothleyohola's column then was in the Cherokee Nation, sheltered by James McDaniel, a Cherokee unhappy with the Confederate alliance. He was not the only Cherokee that disliked the alliance. The day before Chusto-talasah 400 Cherokees in Drew's Regiment were persuaded to change sides. Most were full-bloods, who had enlisted to protect the Indian Territory from invaders, not to fight other Indians, especially the full-blood Creek and Seminole traditionalists that made up Opothleyohola's band.

Chusto-talasah flushed Watcher McDonald from neutrality. As Opothleyohola's column fled past his cabin, Watcher gave them what food he could spare. Called to account for supporting "traitors," Watcher took his horse, his rifle, and what possessions he could carry and slipped north.

This pattern was repeated at Chustenahalan on December 26, 1861, which was fought near Tulsey Town (today's Tulsa). The pro-Union Indians picked a good defensive position, which the Confederate forces attacked. By this time, the loyalists were running low on ammunition. Additionally, their families were worn out by six weeks' flight in winter conditions and had abandoned many of the supply wagons. The result was a rout. Reinforced still further and with additional troops from

Confederate prisoner of war camps for Indian Territory prisoners were grim places. Frontier shortages meant both food and clothing was difficult to obtain. Additionally, captured Indians were assumed to be traitors, and kept in bleak conditions such as those pictured here. (Potter Collection)

Texas and Arkansas, the Confederates scattered Opothleyohola's army. They captured "160 women and children, 20 Negroes, 30 wagons, 70 yoke of cattle, about 500 Indian horses, several hundred head of cattle, 100 sheep, and a great quantity of property." Over 300 of the pro-Union warriors were slain on the battlefield.

Indian fighting tactics

These battles represent the final conflicts between Indians fought in their traditional style of warfare. Opothleyohola's force was a traditional Indian army, with men following war leaders they knew and trusted. Although the Confederate Indians were in formally organized units, their officers were men who would have been war leaders a generation earlier. The tactics were more akin to those seen in a fight between Indians – or the bushwhacking and jayhawking that took place in "Bleeding Kansas" – than Civil War battles.

In this campaign Indians on both sides fought in war paint – just as their ancestors had at Horseshoe Bend in 1812. The Indians went into combat shouting war cries. Private James Kearly, of the 6th Texas Cavalry, stated that as his Indian allies charged into the pro-Union Indians, "they slapped their sides and gobbled like turkeys." Captain H.L. Taylor, of the 3rd Texas Cavalry, reported that his opponents made "all sorts of noises, such as crowing, cackling, and yells."

The Indians also scalped dead opponents during these battles. Private Edward Folsum, of the 1st Choctaw and Chickasaw Regiment, in a postwar memoir claimed that he "got the scalp" of two dead foes at the Chusto-talasah. White soldiers in the Trans-Mississippi, especially those belonging to irregular bands on both sides, could be just as barbaric in mutilating their opponents. Texas irregulars were also accused of scalping the enemy dead. Scalping, especially when carried out on white soldiers in battles where the Indians participated, reinforced white prejudices that these Indians, even if Christian and educated, were still savages.

The next campaign in which Indian troops fought illustrated both their strengths and weaknesses as soldiers. An Indian brigade fought at Pea Ridge, Arkansas, in March 1862. Like white militia units Indian

soldiers could fight tenaciously in defense of their homes, but often proved reluctant warriors when moved out of their own neighborhood. One Indian regiment at Pea Ridge – the Cherokee Drew's Mounted Rifles – fell into that category. They fought tentatively on the first day of the battle, and then withdrew on the second. Several other Indian regiments, including one Creek regiment and the Choctaw and Chickasaw regiments either refused to leave the Indian Territory, or moved too slowly to reach the scene before the battle was decided.

Even when the Indian troops proved eager fighters, they were not always efficient soldiers. Chilly McIntosh's Creek Regiment and the Cherokee Watie's Mounted Rifles welcomed the Pea Ridge campaign as an opportunity to show that they were worthwhile allies of the Confederacy. They made a colorful appearance. A member of the 1st Missouri Brigade wrote, "They came riding into camp yelling forth a wild war whoop that startled the army. Their faces were painted, for they were on the 'warpath.'"

During the battle the two Cherokee regiments – perhaps 1,000-strong, along with 200 Texas cavalry – charged and took a three-gun Union artillery battery. They swept out of the woods, knocking down a fence in front of them, and charged across the field, swarming over a three-gun battery before the startled crews could respond. It was a magnificent feat of arms. The artillerymen fled with their horses, leaving the guns behind unspiked.

At this point experienced, disciplined troops would have established security, or continued the pursuit of their fleeing enemy. The Cherokees did neither. Instead they milled around the guns they had taken, examining their prizes and collecting souvenirs. Others exalted in having survived, yelling and whooping victoriously. It was a normal reaction for green troops after a first experience of combat, and one that was often repeated in that first year of war.

Some wasted time scalping the dead. Of the 25 bodies later found around the guns, eight had been scalped. Drew's full-bloods blamed Watie's mixed-bloods, who in turn blamed the full-bloods. Some Union survivors claimed that that they saw the Texans scalping bodies. All three groups had probably been guilty to some degree.

Indians also assisted the Union Army in Virginia. This photograph shows some of the Pawmunkey Indians that served as scouts and river pilots on the James River. (Library of Congress, Prints and Photographs Division)

The failure of their officers to take charge of the situation cost them the fruits of their victory. While they were celebrating, Union officers deployed two additional batteries and supporting infantry to retake the guns. When the Union batteries opened fire, the soldiers of the Confederate brigade panicked and fled back to the woods where they had started, leaving the three guns of the battery behind.

Panic is the appropriate word for what happened. Less than an hour earlier these troops boldly charged across an open field to take the battery. Disorganized by victory, they were startled into retreat by an unexpected bombardment. Once in the trees, they steadied, dismounting and returning fire from the cover of woods. They fought hard for the rest of the afternoon, but never recovered the guns.

It was a pattern that recurred throughout the rest of the war by Indian troops on both sides of the conflict in the Indian Territory. When they could fight using terrain for cover, they fought tenaciously and held ground doggedly. In a charge – unless faced by a steady and disciplined infantry line – they were invincible. From ambush they were deadly. They were almost arrogantly confident when attacking. But they lacked the training to fight in a line in the open, and the discipline to conduct a rearguard action. As a result, whether the Indian regiments were the best troops available – or the worst – depended entirely on the situation to which they were committed.

Pea Ridge also highlighted another aspect of the Indians in combat. They hated artillery fire, and avoided artillery when they could. While in Kansas trying to interest the whites in an expedition to retake the Indian Territory, Opothleyohola told the United States Army "you must bring us down wagons that shoot." Muskogee lacked a word for artillery, so the chief couched his request in a transliteration of the native term for cannon, but he knew that whoever brought artillery would have an advantage on the battlefield.

The Indians' attitude was sensible and shared by frontier white units that fought on both sides in the Indian Territory. Artillery was the battlefield's wholesale killer. But it limited the effectiveness of Indian troops. When a battery opened fire, the side receiving fire took it as a

The battle of Pea Ridge was the first major appearance of organized Indian units outside of the Indian Territory. Their presence was one of the factors that led Union leaders to authorize the formation of the Union Indian regiments. (Author's collection)

signal to find a new direction to attack, ruining an attack's momentum. A few guns resolutely handled gave a column protection disproportionate to their actual battlefield effectiveness.

The ambush of the *J.R.Williams*

The capture and destruction of the steamboat *J.R.Williams* illustrates the strengths and weaknesses of the Indian soldiers on both sides of the conflict. The *J.R.Williams* was transporting supplies from Fort Smith in Arkansas to Fort Gibson in the Cherokee Nation. The steamboat carried no munitions, but it carried enough food and clothing to free the Union from its dependence on the overland supply line route from Fort Scott for a year, and this in turn would have enabled the troops guarding that line to conduct offensive operations against Confederate-controlled sections of the Indian Territory.

Stand Watie planned and executed an ambush of the boat. One month before the water on the Arkansas River was expected to rise high enough to let the boat reach Fort Gibson, Watie began scouting the riverbank seeking the perfect spot to launch an ambush. He found a sharp bend where the channel came close to the southern bank, 50 miles from Fort Smith. Then, he sent scouts to watch the boat. The day before it was apparent that the *J.R.Williams* was going to sail, he sent three small field pieces and 400 men to the ambush site. He also sent the 200 men of the Cherokee 2nd Mounted Rifles to a spot halfway between the ambush and Fort Smith, to slow any relief force sent to recover the boat.

The ambush was executed perfectly. The artillery caught the boat in a crossfire. Rifle fire from the Indians hidden along the banks threw the Union guard – a company from the 12th Kansas Infantry – into disorder. The pilot steering the boat ran it aground in the ensuing panic. The boat's crew surrendered to the Indians, while the guard swam to the north bank, and then walked to Fort Smith, where they raised the alarm. The next day two regiments were sent from Fort Smith to retake the boat, but their progress slowed to a crawl when they encountered the 2nd Mounted Rifles. Firing from cover, they stalled the Union advance.

Indiscipline then undid Watie's plans. As they unloaded the boat, the food and supplies aboard the *J.R.Williams* proved to be too much of a

Artillery gave the North its margin of victory. Light field pieces, such as this one, permitted the Northern armies to dominate battles and protect supply trains. The Confederate forces in the Indian Territory almost always had fewer artillery pieces than their opponents – if they had any at all. (Library of Congress, Prints and Photographs Division)

temptation for Watie's troops. Their families were starving, and the men loaded up their ponies with food and clothing, then melted away, taking a few days' unofficial leave to take the windfall to their families. By dark Watie's 400 men had shrunk to less than 40.

The 2nd Indian Home Guard Regiment was stationed at the Mackay Salt Works, east of Fort Gibson. This was close enough to hear the cannon fire, and a party of Indians was sent to investigate. They found three members of the boat's guard force who had become separated from the rest of their company. The scouts returned with their intelligence. The commander of the 2nd Indian Home Guard reacted promptly. He sent 200 men, one third of his force, to rescue the boat.

An advance guard – perhaps two dozen men – pushed ahead of the main body, reaching the steamboat by mid-morning. Rather than wait for the rest of the party to come up these Union Indians ran a bluff. Hiding along the riverbank, they began to shoot at the Confederate troops on the opposite bank, maintaining as heavy a fire as possible to give the impression that they were a much larger force.

It worked. The wagons from Boggy Depot had not arrived. There were a handful of Confederate troops available. Colonel W.P. Adair, the Cherokee commander of the 2nd Mounted Rifles, reported that he was being hard-pressed by the force from Fort Gibson. Now a new force of unknown size was pressing from the opposite bank. Watie ordered that the steamboat should be burned.

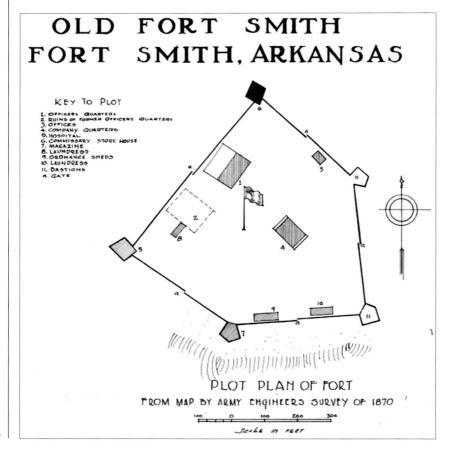

Although steamboats could occasionally reach Fort Gibson, Fort Smith, Arkansas, was the effective head of navigation for the Arkansas River. The US Army built a stockaded fort at that spot prior to the Civil War, which proved to be one of the keys to supplying the Indian Territory. (Library of Congress, Prints and Photographs Division)

The aftermath of the battle illustrated another weakness of Indian troops. They hated picket duty – especially in a retreat. To cover the withdrawal of his artillery, Stand Watie directed Lt. George Grayson to "furnish a sentinel of a suitable number of trusty men to remain and stand watch until *sun down* … in case the enemy appeared in pursuit … to give the alarm." Grayson further stated in his memoirs "… as I had expected, I failed to get a single man to remain." With the pride of youth, Grayson maintained the picket single-handed until sundown, one scared youth upholding what he felt to be the honor of his regiment and his tribe.

Combat was a more personal matter for the Indians than it would be for most of the soldiers in the Civil War. Both George and Watcher would have known some of the men that they fought against, and sometimes killed. Legus Perryman, who served as a sergeant in the 1st Indian Home Guard, remarked about one skirmish, "… we slew about 30 men of the rebels and lost two of our own. Among the dead rebels we found one we knew by name, Walter Mellon."

As raiders they could be invincible. In September 1864, General Gano took 2,000 men (including 800 men from Stand Watie's brigade) on a sweep into the northern half of the Indian Territory. Watie's force was made up of five Indian regiments: two Creek, two Cherokee, and one Seminole. By this stage in the war the Confederate Indian regiments had shrunk to between 125 to 200 men each, but the men that remained were veterans and fighters.

They swept into unprepared Union positions like a cyclone. On September 16, the column destroyed a hay party near the Verdigris River. They moved up to Cabin Creek, and in the pre-dawn hours of the 19th attacked a supply train there. Major Henry Hopkins of the 2nd Kansas Cavalry reported, "At 1 o'clock the enemy opened with artillery and small arms and moved upon my lines with a yell." George Grayson continues the account from the Confederate side: "The enemy did not hold out long but began giving way before our fire, when our Seminole contingent made a rush to deliver an attack in the right, where no fighting had been done."

The civilian teamsters panicked, and attempted to flee. In the process they broke wagon tongues, and stampeded oxen teams. Some of the few that did get moving drove their wagons off a cliff, destroying the wagons and killing the drivers. The Union troops – which included 140 Cherokees and Creeks from the 2nd and 3rd Indian Home Guard – fell back into a stockade near the train, but evacuated after the Confederate troops began shelling it. The Union responded in force the next day, but by then Confederates had destroyed the train: 300 wagons loaded with supplies for Fort Gibson.

The raiders continued their sweep, finally arriving back in Confederate lines two weeks later. In tow they had some 80 captured wagons. The raid's commander, Richard M. Gano, described the results: "We were out fourteen days, marched over 400 miles, killed 97, wounded many, captured 111 prisoners, burned 6,000 tons of hay, and all the reapers and mowers – destroyed altogether from Federals $1,500,000 of property, bringing safely into our lines nearly one-third of that amount (estimated in greenbacks). Our total loss was 6 killed, 48 wounded."

Whatever flaws they had as soldiers, most of which were due to lack of training, the Indians were undoubtedly fighters.

COLLECTING, MUSEUMS, AND RE-ENACTMENT

Collecting memorabilia of the Indian Territory in the Civil War is a challenge. The destruction that took place eliminated most of the prewar artifacts. The few photographs from that region that predate the Civil War survived because their owners evacuated their possessions to Texas early on, and few had the foresight to do that. Weapons, equipment, and items such as battle flags were scarce to begin with, and fared badly with time. Those that escaped time's ravages are now in museums.

The best place to view the remaining artifacts of the Civil War in the Indian Territory is through the various museums and historical sites maintained by the Oklahoma Historical Society (http://www.ok-history.mus.ok.us/mas/maspage.htm). Most of the artifacts are in the Oklahoma Museum of History, although some are on display at the various historical sites around the state. Places such as Fort Gibson, Fort Towson, Fort Washita, and Fort Arbuckle are now historical sites maintained by the Oklahoma Historical Society, as is the Honey Springs battlefield.

Another good resource is the Cherokee Heritage Center (http://www.cherokeeheritage.org) at Park Hill, Oklahoma, with a small collection of Civil War memorabilia, including much of the surviving documents from that era. The Museum of the Cherokee Indian also has some material associated with the Cherokees in the Civil War, although their focus is more on the Thomas Legion, a unit with one battalion of Eastern Branch Cherokees that evaded the Trail of Tears and remained in North Carolina.

A final resource is the Civil War in the Indian Territory Message Board (http://history-sites.com/mb/cw/itcwmb). It is an excellent place to gain and exchange information about the Civil War in the Indian Territory.

A Union Indian who was wounded in battle would most likely have been taken to an open field aid station like this one, for treatment of his wounds. Removal of injured limbs on site was not uncommon. (Library of Congress, Prints and Photographs Division)

BIBLIOGRAPHY

Abel, Annie Heloise, *The Slaveholding Indians: Vol I: As Slaveholder and Secessionist*, Arthur H. Clark Co., Cleveland, OH (1915)

Abel, Annie Heloise, *The Slaveholding Indians: Vol II: As Participant in the Civil War*, Arthur H. Clark Co., Cleveland, OH (1919)

Abel, Annie Heloise, *The Slaveholding Indians: Vol III: Under Reconstruction*, Arthur H Clark Co., Cleveland, OH (1925)

Britton, Wiley, *The Union Indian Brigade in the Civil War*, Franklin Hudson Publishing, Kansas City, MO (1921)

Dale, Edward E., *Cherokee Cavaliers: Forty Years of Cherokee History as Told in the Correspondence of the Ridge-Watie-Boudinot Family*, University of Oklahoma Press, Norman, OK (1939)

Dyer, Frederick H., *A Compendium of the War of the Rebellion, Compiled and Arranged from Official Records of the Federal and Confederate Armies, Reports of the Adjutant Generals of the Several States, the Army Registers and Other Reliable Documents and Sources in 3 Volumes*, Dyer Publishing Co., Des Moines (1908)

Edwards, Whit, *The Prairie Was On Fire: Eyewitness Accounts of the Civil War, Oklahoma Historical Society*, Oklahoma City, OK (2001)

Frazer, Robert W., *Forts of the West*, University of Oklahoma Press, Norman, OK (1965)

Gaines, Craig W., *The Confederate Cherokees: John Drew's Regiment of Mounted Rifles*, Louisiana State University Press, Baton Rouge, LA (1989)

Grayson, G.W., *A Creek Warrior for the Confederacy: The Autobiography of Chief G.W. Grayson*, University of Oklahoma Press, Norman, OK (1988)

Hauptman, Laurence M., *Between Two Fires: American Indians in the Civil War*, The Free Press, New York, NY (1995)

Halliburton, R. Jr., *Red over Black: Black Slavery Among the Cherokee Indians*, Greenwood Press, Westport, Conn. (1977)

Kievit, Joyce Ann., "Dissention in the Cherokee Nation 1860 to 1866", UH-CL theses. Houston, TX (1992)

Knight, Wilfred Red Fox, *Stand Watie and the Confederate Indian Nations*, A.H. Clark, Co., Glendale, CA (1988)

McBride, Lela, *Opothleyaholo and the Loyal Muskogees: Their Flight to Kansas in the Civil War*, McFarland and Co., Jefferson, NC (2000)

Sifakis, Stewart, *Compendium of the Confederate Armies: Kentucky, Maryland, Missouri, the Confederate Units and the Indian Units*, Facts on File, New York, NY (1993)

White, Christine Schulz, and White, Benton R., *Now the Wolf Has Come: The Creek Nation in the Civil War*, Texas, A&M University Press, College Station, TX (1996)

US War Dept., *The War of the Rebellion: A Compilation of the Official Records of the Union and Confederate Armies*, 128v. Washington, DC: GPO, 1880–1901 (Especially Series I, Vol. 1, 4, 8, 13, 21, 34, and 41)

US Navy Dept., *Official Records of the Union and Confederate Navies in the War of the Rebellion*, 31v. Washington, DC: GPO (1922)

Web Resources

The Civil War Soldiers and Sailors System, National Park Service lists information about units, individual soldiers, and battles. (http://www.itd.nps.gov/cwss/index.html)

The Prints and Photographs Online Catalog (PPOC), United States Library of Congress is an unrivaled visual resource of the era. (http://www.loc.gov/rr/print/catalog.html)

COLOR PLATE COMMENTARY

A: PRIVATE, UNION INDIAN BRIGADE, 1862

Indians enlisting in the Union Army often lacked equipment or modern weapons. In 1862, upon joining they were issued a Hardee hat, a four-button sack coat, a rifle, and a cartridge box in which to store ammunition, and the tools for the weapon. Initially they fought in civilian trousers and shirts, and scrounged their own haversack and knapsack. They rode to war on their own mounts – generally a pony or a mustang – and brought their own saddle and tack.

The Union Indians were generally those following the traditional Indian ways, which showed in their dress. They preferred wearing moccasins to shoes or boots, and added feathers to their Hardee hats. Some, especially Creek and Seminole Indians, went into battle wearing war paint, although as the war continued war paint appeared less.

This soldier belongs to the 1st Indian Home Guard Regiment and is armed with the 1817 model rifled musket. Additional weapons and rifles issued to the other regiments are shown in the margin of the plate: 1. Prussian rifle; 2. Mississippi rifle; 3. tomahawk; 4. side knives; 5. .36 cal. 1851 Navy Colt revolver.

Tools for the 1817 rifle are shown at the foot of plate A: 6. ladle for holding molten lead; 7. powder flask; 8. bullet mold; 9. cartridge box; 10. lead for bullets; 11. pricker.

Wiley Britton, who fought alongside the Union Indian Brigade, described them: "Care was not taken to see to it that the clothing issued to the Indian soldiers fitted properly … giving the Indian soldier a comical appearance mounted on their ponies with badly fitted clothing and wearing 'Hancock' [Hardee] hats, with their long black hair falling over their shoulders and legs astride their mounts coming down to the ground. But the comical appearance did not prevent them from shooting straight when skirmishing with the foe."

B: RECRUITING

This plate illustrates the different approaches to recruiting for the Confederacy and Union.

Confederate regiments (*top*) were raised by Indian nations. The tribal government issued a call for its citizens to report to a government building, such as an Agency building, a schoolhouse, a church, or in this case the Chickasaw Council House, where the Chickasaw legislature met. It was a scene similar to those seen throughout the United States, both North and South. A local Indian politician or possibly a member of the tribal police – "the light horse," as they were termed – would exhort the citizens to join. Then, those willing, often young men looking for adventure, or middle-aged planters worried about the effects of abolition on their property, enrolled in one of the companies of the regiment. Men brought their own weapons, if they had them. Joining without arms often meant a long wait in a barracks until an issue weapon trickled in from Texas or Arkansas.

The first obstacle that pro-Union Indians faced (*below*) was being permitted to fight. The North resisted organizing Indian units – especially among refugees from the Indian Territory – until the spring of 1862. (Indians from Kansas were allowed to join Kansas state cavalry regiments, especially those short

The Civil War in the Trans-Mississippi region was total war. Stealing supplies from civilian supporters of the other side was a common occurrence in the Indian Territory and the surrounding states, both Union and Confederate. (Potter Collection)

of men.) When Washington finally consented, the first two regiments were organized from the remnants of Opothleyohola's loyalist band. This included slaves that had run away from Indian masters. These Indians had lost most of their possessions when the Confederates drove them out of the territory in December 1861. They survived a winter of neglect by the Federal government, which issued condemned tents, old blankets, and rotten food to the refugees. Necessity encouraged many to join the Union Army, as they were reduced to rags, if that. The opportunity to reclaim by arms the lands they had lost to their Confederate cousins also prompted them to enlist.

C: OUTFITTING THE INDIAN SOLDIER – THE TRANS-MISSISSIPPI WAY

One of the most daring exploits of the Civil War was the seizure of the steamboat *J.R.Williams* by a force of Confederate Indians led by the redoubtable Stand Watie. The steamboat was headed to Fort Gibson with 500 barrels of flour, 16,000lb of bacon, 20 sacks of coffee, 15 barrels of brown sugar, and fresh uniforms for the garrison. Watie successfully trapped the boat with an artillery ambush at a bend in the river. The guard aboard the *J.R.Williams* panicked, and the pilot ran the ship aground on the southern side of the river, where Watie's men swarmed aboard.

Except for denying the Union the supplies, the Confederate Army failed to capitalize on their windfall. In Stand Watie's words this prize "was very acceptable to the boys, but has turned out to be a disadvantage to the command, as the greater portions of the Creeks and Seminoles immediately broke off to carry their booty home." Possibly a similar percentage of Cherokees also left, but Watie – a Cherokee – said nothing about them. Left with only a few men, he burned the *J.R.Williams*, and destroyed most of the supplies when the Union's 2nd Indian Home Guard Regiment attempted to recapture the steamboat.

For individual soldiers of Watie's force, the ship yielded a bounty for them and their families. This plate shows how they loaded their mounts with all the food they could carry. While the officers were preoccupied, some groups also took the initiative to examine the captured stores privately, and to "acquire" clothing and equipment needed to complete their outfit. Confederate Indian Regiments lacked "standard" issues but the man on the right now has a typical outfit:

- Socks
- Drawers
- Canteen
- Cartridge box
- Two coats
- Shoes
- Washcloth and towel
- Hat
- Knapsack
- Shirts
- Personal possessions – a razor, a Bible, a small mirror, a picture of his sweetheart.

D: THE BATTLE OF CHUSTENAHALAN, DECEMBER 26, 1861

Chustenahalan underscored the biggest weakness of the traditionalist Indians who remained loyal to the North. Their army was unorganized, with Indians and runaway slaves united

The locks of two rifles assembled at the Tyler Armory in Tyler, Texas. The majority of arms used by Confederate Indians that were issued rather than brought from home were "Texas" rifles. (Smith County Historical Society)

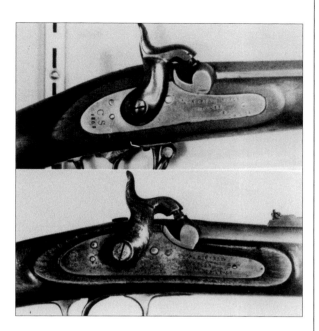

only by an unwillingness to fight the United States. They needed firearms to exist, but could not produce the gunpowder these weapons used. Earlier battles at Round Mountain and Chusto-talasah (Bird Creek) almost exhausted their original supplies. The Confederate Indians fell back on their depots and got more, but the Union loyalists lacked sources for resupply.

Before the battle the loyalists pooled what gunpowder they had and gave it to their best marksmen. Except for this handful, the force was reduced to knives, axes, and clubs. The Confederate Indians, armed with rifles and ample ammunition quickly scattered the Union forces, who broke into small groups in an attempt to evade the pursuing Confederates.

It became a deadly game of hide-and-seek. Groups of a dozen mounted Confederates – mixed groups of Southern Indians and Texas cavalry – hunted through the countryside seeking pairs and trios of Northern Indians, who were typically on foot. If caught, all the Northern warriors could do was sell their lives as dearly as possible. The escaping Northern Indians relied on concealment, rather than combat to survive.

This plate shows one incident. Two loyal sharpshooters – Creeks skilled with firearms – and a runaway slave armed with a two-handed axe, are watching the progress of a Confederate search party across the creek from their position.

Indians on both sides wore war paint in this battle. The solely black war paint shows that the Creek believes he is fighting for survival. Neither side had uniforms. The Confederates tied a white or red string around their right upper arms for identification. Both wore the kind of clothing they would normally wear for work outdoors in cold weather. The loyalists, however, lacked adequate clothing, having lost their baggage.

Finding sufficient fodder was always a challenge. It required both Union and Confederate armies to send out hay-gathering parties, which were vulnerable to ambush. (Library of Congress, Prints and Photographs Division)

E: FORT GIBSON, JUNE 1863

Getting a horse shod was not a glamorous aspect of military life, but was critical to a horse's endurance and its rider's well-being. The military posts in the Indian Territory provided a place where such mundane but necessary tasks could be done. Two of the most important buildings in Fort Gibson were its bakery and blacksmith shop. The bakery fed both the garrison and the Indian civilian refugees that camped around the post. The blacksmith shop kept metal equipment – from wagon hardware to horseshoes – in fighting condition.

The Union Indian regiments enrolled as infantry, but fought mounted when possible. The mounts were the property of the riders and generally the Indians of the region rode plains ponies or mustangs. Brightly colored pinto, paints, and appaloosa horses which were short and tough were favored by the Creeks, Seminoles, and Osage who made up much of the 1st Regiment.

The Indians brought their own tack with them, too. Much of their equipment, like the saddle in the foreground, was made by the owner, in this case, of rawhide and wood. The corporal holding his newly shod horse (*left*) has acquired an army-issue saddle blanket.

The farrier shoeing the horses is a white soldier, part of Fort Gibson's garrison. While the local blacksmith and farrier in a Cherokee or Creek town would be an Indian, typically a mixed-blood, when these tradesmen joined the Union Army they were usually assigned to a line company as riflemen.

The private waiting to get his horse shod (*center*) is a member of the Kee-too-wah, an abolitionist society formed by full-blooded Cherokees. Members wore a corn shuck on their chest or in their hair, or – as in this case – placed a pair of crossed pins on the collar of their coat.

F: RAID ON A HAY PARTY, 1864

After their defeat at Honey Springs, Confederate forces were reduced to the role of guerrillas and raiders. The Confederate Indians proved adept at both. On September 16, 1864, Confederate forces including the Indian Brigade commanded by Stand Watie, surprised a hay party sent out from Fort Gibson, and escorted by two companies of the 2nd Kansas Cavalry and one company of the 79th US Colored Troops (formerly the 1st Kansas Infantry (Colored)). Unfortunately, the black troops were also expected to help harvest hay – which put the main defense of the party in the hands of the 80 men of the 2nd Kansas Cavalry. The party was scattered over a three-square-mile area of prairie near the Grand Timber River, 15 miles west of Fort Gibson. The terrain was flat, and cut by shallow pools that ranged from a few yards to 50 yards long and about 2 feet deep.

The Confederate force probably numbered 1,200, and they swept across the plain like a scythe. The Kansas Cavalry dismounted and attempted to fight on foot (they were armed with repeating breechloaders) but failed to hold their ground. The commander finally ordered his men to mount and charge the weakest point of the Confederate line. Of the 65 troopers that attempted the charge, only 15 broke through. The rest were killed or captured.

The black troops, from whom no surrender was accepted, fought until overwhelmed. They used the lagoons as strongpoints, and held the Confederates for two hours, until they ran out of ammunition. Forty were butchered as they attempted to flee. Ten escaped, either hiding in the tall grass, or by hiding themselves in the lagoons. The Confederates burned the hay and smashed the harvesting machines.

This plate shows the onset of the attack, with the Confederate line charging down on the unprepared harvesters.

G: HOMECOMING, 1865

The Civil War left the Indian Territory in ruins. At the end of the war, perhaps one-sixth of its inhabitants were dead; one-third of the wives were widows; one-sixth of the children were orphans with no parents, and almost as many were fatherless. Almost every barn, house, store, and public building in the Indian Territory had been burned down. The only exceptions were places like the Armstrong Academy that had been used as military strongpoints.

Additionally, the nations were bankrupt. The public treasuries had been spent on the war. Monies owed the Tribes for their Eastern lands by the federal government were forfeit. Since the Indian Nations had formally declared war on

Most Indians had homes that were less grand than the multi-story mansions of Park Hill. The average Cherokee lived in "dog trots" or log cabins such as the one pictured here. Built prior to the Civil War, it was still being used as a home in 1936, when it was photographed by the Historical Architecture and Buildings Survey. (Library of Congress, Prints and Photographs Division)

the United States, peace could only be concluded with formal treaties – treaties in which the Indian Nations forfeited much of their sovereignty, surrendered claims to land, and accepted the relocation of new tribes into the Territory.

What was left? Rebuilding. Some, like the Union veteran and Confederate veteran in this plate, were able to put their differences behind them and work together. Others confined their future disputes to the political arena. Still others carried grudges into peacetime, especially among the Creeks and Seminoles. The Delaware relocated from the Washita Agency to the northern part of the Cherokee Nation, where the Kansas branch of the tribe joined them.

For most, the immediate problem was getting a roof over their heads – something more substantial than a lean-to made from a dog-tent, which these former enemies are sharing. Fortunately, the eastern half of the Indian Territory still had plenty of timber after the Civil War. From that you could make the type of log cottage that these cousins are assembling in the plate. The gaps between the logs were filled with mortar or clay, yielding a building that stayed warm in the winter and cool in the summer.

H: SERGEANT, CHEROKEE 1ST MOUNTED RIFLES, 1864

Men such as the sergeant in this plate, formed the rigid backbone that kept the Southern Indians fighting. His equipment was inferior to that of his Union Indian counterpart, except for those pieces that he raided from Northern supply trains or scavenged off the battlefield. By 1864 at least part of what he wore originally came from a Union commissary; the red stripes of this man's trousers show that they were intended for use by a Union artilleryman. The rest of his clothing is civilian, the remains of what he had when he enlisted, although a wife or a fiancée probably added the sergeant's stripes on the civilian jacket.

His main weapon was most likely a sawn-off shotgun (**3**). The barrel has been shortened to allow it to be more easily used while mounted, and the weapon probably came from his farm. Other weapons commonly used by these troops included the Texas rifle (**1**) and hunting rifles such as this Kentucky rifle (**2**). He is also armed with a pair of Colt Navy revolvers (**5** and **6**) – probably collected on the battlefield – and the ubiquitous Bowie, or side-knife, carried by most Confederates, white or Indian (**4**).

His mount is a Chickasaw, a breed developed by the Chickasaw Indians from horses captured from the Spanish in the 1500s. The breed is extremely hardy, and capable of great bursts of speed over short distances, making it an ideal raider's mount in broken country.

The flag is the banner of the Cherokee 1st Mounted Rifles. This unit started as a volunteer Confederate force raised by Stand Watie in 1861 and was redesignated after the original Cherokee 1st Mounted Rifles (Drew's Rifles) deserted to the Union in 1862. The banner uses the 1861 Confederate flag as a template with a cross of five red stars inside the circle of white stars. The white stars represented the states of the Confederacy while the red stars symbolized the Five Civilized Nations that allied themselves with the South.

The battle flag of the 1st Cherokee Volunteers as it appears today. (Cherokee Heritage Center)

INDEX